The Art of SLOW TRAVEL

See the World and Savor the Journey

On a Budget

Bhavana Gesota

The Art of Slow Travel: See the World and Savor the Journey On a Budget

First edition 2021
ISBN: 978-1-7360743-0-5 (Paperback)
Publisher: Bhavana Gesota
San Francisco, California, USA

For permissions and inquiry contact: bhavanagesota@gmail.com

DISCLAIMER

The information presented in this book is a collection of anecdotes, advice, and opinions from a person who has lived in different countries for different lengths of time and talked to several others who have done the same; however, none of it is guaranteed to be current or without fault.

Nothing in this book should be construed as legal, financial, or medical advice that should be taken without secondary consideration. Prices, visa requirements, and exchange rates are in constant flux. Anything written in these pages is subject to change, so always verify the tips from this book before basing any decisions on them.

DOWNLOAD YOUR FREE GIFT

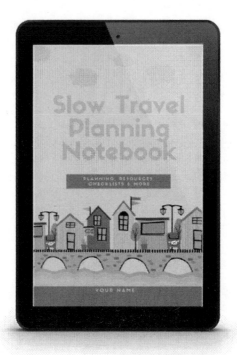

I believe being actively engaged in planning your slow travel journey paves the way to getting the most out of the experience. This notebook will give you the space to pause, ponder, and scribble about the critical points and questions you'll discover throughout this book. It also includes a complete resource list and a planning and packing checklist that you can use to check off items as you plan and pack for your travel.

Don't forget to return to my website for updated versions from time to time. Because, in travel, there is no full-stop. Only a new paragraph added or a section deleted.

Go to the link below to download your FREE Slow Travel Planning Notebook now!

<u>author.bhavanagesota.com/stpn</u>

CONTENTS

Section IV - In A Relationship

Chapter 1

How It All Began

A message beeped on my phone. "Hey, where are you now?" It was Sudha, a friend from California, checking in.

"I'm still in Iquitos in Peru."

"Oh! I didn't realize that you were still there. How much longer are you planning to stay there?"

"Four more months, I think."

"Four more months? Wow! I wish I could live your life!" she texted back.

Over the years, this type of conversation has become quite common with friends and family. *Where are you now? How long are you staying there? What are you doing there? Aren't you scared of traveling alone?*

These kinds of repetitive questions used to be annoying at first. But later, I realized that they were trying to live vicariously through me and my adventures across the globe as they didn't believe that they could slow travel as I do.

"But you can! If I can do this, so can *you!*" I tell them.

"How do you go about it?" is always the follow-up question.

Well, *that* is precisely what I want to show you in this book.

I can say that because from 1995 until 2020, I have lived in nine countries—not counting India, my birth country—worked in seven of them, and traveled to twenty-two more over five continents.

During this grand earth-walk, I have seen some of the most breathtaking sights and come across different cultures and spiritual beliefs, which at times have been challenging and contradictory. I have learned new languages and crossed paths with people from different walks of life, some of whom have become lifelong friends. These experiences have provided me with plenty of food for reflection and a lived understanding of the shared humanity we inhabit.

 Once the layers are peeled away, we all have the same needs, the same desires, and the same shadows.

Imagine...

A ten-year-old girl in pigtails and glasses, hanging around outside the Mumbai airport with her extended family members. A chaotic scene of honking cars and taxis. The smell of humidity clinging to the skin as if one had just stepped out of a sauna. A crowd swarmed over each other as though the airport was a bustling bazaar. Occasionally a breeze of fresh air provided relief from the heavy smell of sweat permeating the air. It was 10 p.m. in peak Mumbai summer. The little girl had come to bid farewell to her *nanima**, who was leaving for the USA.

Somewhere amidst the cheerful banter and hugs, from the corner of her eye, she spotted a group of backpackers nearby. Curious, she turned her gaze in their direction. Backpacks on their shoulders, water bottles hanging from one side, shoes hanging from the other, a rolled-up sleeping bag perched on top. They were wearing worn-out shorts, T-shirts, and dust-covered sandals. It seemed that they had been on the road for a while. Although she couldn't fully understand what they were saying in their thick Australian accents, she managed to catch a few words here and there. She understood that they had been backpacking in India for a year and were now heading home to Australia.

In that instant, a thought flashed through her mind:

One day, I am going to do the same.

---

*   *nanima,* maternal grandmother in Gujarati

She turned her head as her *nanima* called out to give her a final hug before entering the airport. She promised to write letters in *Gujarati*.

It was the first time she had come this close to people from a distant land. This incident piqued her curiosity further. She found comfort in her world atlas and old editions of National Geographic from the local library. It was a time when there was no internet or TV. Often while sitting on the verandah railing under the jasmine vine, she would gaze up at the moon and ask it what it was like on the other side of the world. She dreamt of visiting those faraway lands someday.

That girl was me.

Fast Forward to the Present

Sudha's text message acted like a trigger to begin what I had been postponing. The first semblance of this book began to develop on a few loose A4 size printer papers. It was during an evening laden with rain and thunder in Iquitos, Peru, in 2017. I was sitting on the Dawn of the Amazon Cafe's second-floor terrace located on the boulevard across the Amazon River. Amidst a dinner of baked *tacu tacu*† and *camu camu*‡ juice and fending off a Peruvian man asking me out on a date, I wrote about six pages meant to be a series of blog posts titled *How to Ground on the Nomadic Track*.

I saved these pages intending to continue back at the artists' residency in Tarapoto but never did. Very quickly, 2017 turned into 2020. An inspiration to write a book instead of a series of blog posts arrived on the beach of Puerto Escondido, Mexico. So did COVID-19.

I almost swept the few pages I had started into a cyber-corner on my Mac. Then I realized that, through my personal experiences, I wanted to write a book that spoke to an audience that seeks to deepen their connection with themselves and the world through

---

* *Gujarati*, an Indo-Aryan language native to the state of Gujarat in India and one of India's official languages
† *tacu tacu*, a Peruvian dish of leftover rice and canary beans fried on a skillet to make a patty
‡ *camu camu*, a berry native to the Amazon rainforest

slow travel. I also realized that it is because of COVID-19 and the restrictions placed on travel that it is indeed the right time to re-think travel as we emerge into the new normal. Slow travel, a different way of traveling, felt even more appropriate than ever before.

I revived the book.

What This Book Is About

Have you ever wondered how some people seem to be traveling and living in different parts of the world for months or even years at a time? But these individuals aren't retired, and they're certainly not millionaires.

You dream of being able to do the same. You want to set foot on that long slow travel road. But fears, doubts, and myths prevent you from taking that leap.

Here are the eight most common fears, doubts, and myths about slow travel I have come across, which keep people locked into a state of inaction. These include my own when I first started to travel against the well-meaning advice and warnings from concerned friends and family.

#1 It costs a fortune to slow travel long-term. You have to be retired or have some investment/trust funds.

#2 It's dangerous to travel—especially as a solo woman.

#3 I'm too old to go on a slow travel trip.

#4 It's impossible to pick back up where I left off in my career upon return. Being out of sight is being out of mind in the professional world.

#5 Organizing a long slow travel trip is a daunting process.

#6 Traveling solo is lonely.

#7 Will I be able to cope if things don't go according to plan?

#8 I feel unequipped to handle being outside of my comfort zone.

At this time, I will ask you a question.

 Which is stronger?

Your desire to set foot on the slow road?

Or

Your fears, doubts, and myths?

If this is something you genuinely want to do, then you are reading the right book. This book *is* about helping you overcome these fears, doubts, and myths by providing you with practical advice, tips, resources, and anecdotes from my own slow travels.

#1 This book encompasses all aspects of slow travel from planning, organizing finances, finding accommodation, to landing, making new friends, avoiding common pitfalls, and finding your footing in your new life in a new country in a step-by-step manner.

#2 It includes the different ways by which you can earn a living while traveling—an intimidating obstacle that stops many from taking this leap.

#3 It discusses the challenges we face on the slow travel road and how to overcome them. Yes! Challenges. Because like anything else in life that is worth doing, slow traveling will come with its own set of challenges.

#4 Finally, it points out what and how to precisely research while giving you a ton of resources.

What this book is *not* about:

#1 It's not destination-specific. If you want to learn everything about traveling in Argentina, let's say, this is not the right book.

#2 It is also not specific to traveling by RV, with children, sailing across the seas, biking across continents, etc., since I lack the experience to write about them in detail.

Despite this, there are many aspects of slow travel that remain the same. I can guarantee that what I share throughout this book will be useful and relevant for all travelers.

I recently met Jane, a seventy-three-year-old British woman. She started her solo slow travel trails at the ripe age of sixty. With a youthful sparkle in her eyes, she demurely announced her next trip over a cup of hot chocolate in a café—climb Mt. Everest in 2021 and live in Nepal for six months! My jaw dropped in awe. Many like her don't let their age discourage them from pursuing their dreams. They *choose* to live a life full of curiosity and enthusiasm rather than a life diminished by old age.

Youth is not a prerequisite to travel. Only the spirit of wanderlust is.

The Art of Slow Travel: See the World and Savor the Journey On a Budget is a comprehensive one-stop-shop that dives into the nuts and bolts of slow travel to inspire and help you get started. You will save lots of time and hassle in the process. So, toss your fears, doubts, and myths out of the window and make a plan.

 After all, what's your time worth?

SECTION I

FLIRTING WITH THE IDEA

At some point, all the horizontal trips in the world stop compensating for the need to go deep into somewhere challenging and unexpected; movement makes most sense when grounded in stillness. In an age of speed, I began to think, nothing could be more invigorating than going slow. In an age of distraction, nothing could feel more luxurious than paying attention. And in an age of constant movement, nothing is more urgent than sitting still.

Pico Iyer

Chapter 2

What Is Slow Travel?

I couldn't have said it better than Pico Iyer. But let me break it down into a more concrete idea.

Slow Travel is Not

- A checklist of condensed destinations to see within a short period of time.
- A mind *filled* with things to do.
- The mantra "doing more is better."
- Fixed plans accompanied by a detailed itinerary.
- A break or a holiday from everyday life and routine.

Slow Travel is

- Few fixed plans and more time and space for serendipity.
- An ethos of simplicity and mindfulness.
- The mantra "doing less is more."
- Soaking in the local flavors and culture at your own pace.
- As much of an inner journey as it is an outer journey.

There is no official definition for slow travel, but I posit:

 Slow travel is an offbeat, slow, and responsible manner of travel in which everyday life unfolds within the framework of a different culture.

Wanting to gain a broader sense of what slow travel is, I asked some fellow slow travelers what it meant to them.

Cassi from the U.K started to travel in 2017. What began as a three-month trip through three countries turned into an ongoing journey that has yet to reach its end. According to her:

"Slow travel is being in a place long enough to experience it without having a strict itinerary. It isn't about seeing everything but experiencing the soul of a place."

Jeff, an anthropologist who has been practicing slow travel methodologies since 2000, offered his definition:

"For me, slow travel is not hitting the top spots, but staying somewhere long enough to know how people live and even start to live as locals do—mastering local transportation, finding where the good deals are, finding local favorites, and learning what makes the local people special compared to other people around the country...I have often wondered what makes people the same and different, and I enjoy exploring new cultures to see how they solve universal problems in unique ways."

John is an epicurean pizzaiolo, a taco raconteur, and a proud father and husband living the sweet life on Bainbridge Island in Washington State. He described the kind of experiences that make up slow traveling:

"I want to do things like the locals do. I want to pay electric bills, know the servers at my favorite restaurants and bars, and have local friends. For me, traveling at that speed is slow travel, where I can savor all the ingredients, do it myself, even avoid big hotel and restaurant chains, and experience what's best about that place—much in the way the slow food movement exists."

Kriszta felt burnt out after many years of working in corporate culture. She quit her "shiny" management job in the Netherlands in 2019, worked out how to do freelance work remotely, and started to travel.

"Traveling for me is learning the language, the culture, the food, the music, the way of thinking, and how all parts of life are interrelated. In a culture different than mine, slow travel is the only way for me to understand this world and people's motivations and their lifestyles."

Marijntje is from the Netherlands. Her name means little mother

(*Ma*) of the river Rhine (*Rijn*). Her grandmother had always wanted to sail on the Rhine, but passed away just a week before Marijntje was born. Her name holds her grandmother's wish to go on a slow journey. She captures the essence of slow travel very well:

> *"Maybe the essence of slow travel to me is to be somewhere instead of doing a lot of things."*

The impulse to spend time checking off items on a tourist to-do-list is strong when we arrive in a new and unfamiliar place. But slow travel is not about escaping life or taking a short break from the daily humdrum. You are living your life on the slow road. What I find extraordinary is the genuine sense of joy and fulfillment that comes from ordinary everyday experiences in an unfamiliar place and culture.

Come to think of it, weren't our nomadic or seminomadic ancestors slow travelers themselves? They used to travel from place to place in tribes looking for food and shelter. They settled in one place for a while before moving on when survival necessitated it.

Our other ancestors traveled in caravans over long distances, going from one land to another as traders. They exchanged cultures, beliefs, ideas, cuisines, and art with the people of the lands they were passing through along the way. Together they created fusions and wove new threads into the tapestry of their culture. Life did not come to a standstill because they were nomadic. It continued to unfold and evolve on the slow trade road.

Some of us have not changed that much after all. Our nomadic ancestors live on in a small part of our subconscious, fueling the urge to journey to foreign lands, not so much for survival or economic trade but as a rite of passage filled with expansive levels of transformation on many levels. A deep and rich encounter with a new culture whose ideas of living could be, at times, conflicting or contradictory to our own becomes a catalyst to examine and shift our preexisting notions of living. We choose to go on this journey to not only explore a different external world but through this meeting; we seek to uncover facets of our own self.

Slow travel is as much a journey of discovering a new culture as it is about self-discovery.

It can also be understood through the concept of slow food. In slow food, we still eat food, but what we eat and how we eat differs. It rejects fast food, emphasizes eating locally produced fresh food, preserving biodiversity, and encourages us to savor what we eat, not devour it.

Akin to slow food, in slow travel, we still travel, but how we travel and the mindset with which we travel differs from mainstream tourism. Slow travel rejects speed, emphasizes soaking in the local culture, and encourages us to savor the journey, not rush it.

At this point, I ask you to sit back and give it a thought:

 What does slow travel mean to you?
What type of experiences form a slow travel journey?

Conscious Slow Travel

What if, while traveling, we also bring awareness to the choices we make during our travels?

Conscious slow travel is taking slow travel one step further. It is not just about rethinking *how* we travel but also *what* impact our journey has on the local communities, cultures, natural environment, and wildlife we come in contact with. It is about asking meaningful questions and reflecting upon the answers before making decisions.

Such as:

- *When I make a purchase, to whose pocket will the money go? Will it support a local business?*
- *By booking a tour, what environmental hazard am I contributing to? Will my travel endanger natural habitats? Can I help protect that?*
- *When I volunteer for an NGO, does the NGO walk the talk?*
- *Instead of flying, can I take a bus or train?*

👉 *Conscious slow travel is as much about giving back as it is about receiving.*

You might think that this sounds like sustainable travel. It is one and the same minus the fact that sustainable travel is an ideology, whereas conscious slow travel throws the ball back in your court. It asks you to reflect on how *you* can travel sustainably by making responsible choices along the way. It is empowering when you take action instead of just intellectually understanding the concept of sustainable travel.

Why Conscious Slow Travel?

The tourism worldwide statistics and facts report published by Statista on March 31, 2020, states that travel and tourism "made a total contribution (direct, indirect, and induced) of 8.27 trillion U.S. dollars to the global economy in 2017." UNWTO's Tourism Highlights 2017 reported a total of 1.326 million international tourist arrivals in destinations worldwide, "showing a growth of 7% over the previous years." The number of tourists has been estimated to reach 1.8 billion by 2030.

The COVID-19 pandemic is likely going to render this estimate invalid. However, what these reports unarguably illustrate is that the mainstream travel and tourism industry has become far more accessible and affordable to most people. It is no longer a luxury available only to the rich. They also prove that travel and tourism play a large role in the world economy.

Many parts of this world are sustained *solely* by this industry. The absence of this industry places an immense strain on the survival of these communities. We now know this to be an indisputable fact due to the COVID-19 pandemic. On the flip side, this industry also has its downsides. The increase in mainstream travel and tourism places the environment and social fabric of cultures at risk.

As Tim Neville, an American travel writer told **World Nomads** in 2018:

> *The story isn't new, but we wrestle with it every time. A relatively small group of people 'discover' a relatively unknown place that's so fun and beautiful and seemingly rare that they do what any likable human would do—they talk about it. How can you not share the joy? But things can get out of hand quickly, too, and it's a pretty slippery slope. The more people talk, the more the media listens, which makes more people talk, and suddenly, a place is 'ruined.'*

That leads me to what Jane Goodall has rightly said:

> *You cannot get through a single day without having an impact on the world around you. What you do makes a difference, and you have to decide what kind of difference you want to make.*

If we want to preserve the very qualities that we seek and find so alluring in our travels, it is increasingly important to consider the impact that our travels have on our destinations due to our travel choices.

My Conscious Slow Travel Mantra

Here is my 7-point conscious slow travel mantra that I try to adhere to. It is not carved in stone and can change. It provides me with a guideline to do my part and be a conscious drop in this ocean.

#1 I treat travel as a learning opportunity with an open and curious mind.

#2 I travel without the mindset of privilege and entitlement.

#3 I observe and reflect upon the traditions of other cultures, but I will not appropriate them.

#4 I will not treat the local people and their long-held traditions and customs as tourist attractions. I will learn about these ahead of time and become mindful of what is important for the people.

#5 I explore the differing worldviews I encounter and try to understand and accept them even if they may not fit my own.

#6 I choose environmentally friendly options when available.

#7 I follow the motto: "Think globally but act locally."

While this may sound like a lot, it's not. The key is:

 Keep it small, simple, and actionable.

Often times, I have seen that we care so much that we wait around for an opportunity to make a big impact. But small actions make a bigger impact *because* they are immediately actionable. The "Conscious Slow Traveler" section at the end of several chapters makes suggestions on easy-to-do things to get you thinking. While reading them, you might go:

Huh! So why is this specific to slow travel? I can do some of these at home or even when I am going on a short holiday.

I am glad you asked!

Remember what I said earlier about what slow travel is? Life does not stop while on the slow travel track. It only unfolds in the context of a different culture. If you have already been doing many of these at home, remind yourself to continue doing them during your slow travels and find more ways!

 At this point, I invite you to write your own conscious slow travel mantra.

CHAPTER 3

THE WHY, WHERE, HOW & HOW LONG

Images of languid lunches on sun-dappled terraces. Blue and whitewashed houses engulfed by pink bougainvillea vines. The dancing shades of azure blue and clear turquoise waters. Limestone buildings lit up by the setting sun in a city that is more ancient than the word ancient. The romance of being elegantly perched in a city that straddles Asia and Europe. The mysticism of ancient sites of ritual, power, and worship while floating down the Nile pretending to be Cleopatra.

Slow traveling around the Mediterranean was no longer a honeymoon plan reserved for the future but had become a burning desire of the incurable romantic in me. A flirtation had been brewing for several months. On a cold February morning and a dash of reckless abandon later, I secured six months of unpaid sabbatical from the confines of the grey cubicles of my office in Silicon Valley, California. My friends balked at this daredevil decision.

"Do you really think you'll be able to come back to work after taking half a year off? It's career suicide!"

"Can you imagine how much money you will *not* make if you take off like that?"

"Remember to *not* have any regrets later."

I weighed my options:

Being employee #12345678 logging in at 8 a.m. into the binary dullness of a Silicon Valley tech giant.

Or

Free falling on a trip around the Mediterranean Sea.

Need I say which of the two won? My flirtation with the Mediterranean wanted to run its course. And my wanderlust had fueled enough to withstand a heartbreak. After all, what is a romance sans risqué?

It was a soul-searching journey. A time alone to take a step back from my life and career in Silicon Valley. To shed tears in unfamiliar places amongst unfamiliar people for all that I had lost. To celebrate all that I had struggled for and achieved up until then, but most importantly to reexamine my life and replenish my soul.

Soon, I found myself with a backpack, stepping into a world which until then had been confined to my world atlas and National Geographic magazines.

Destination: Traveling overland in Greece, Turkey, Israel, and Egypt over the course of six months.

I sold the majority of my belongings, packed up the rest of my two-bedroom apartment into a 10x20 storage space, and bought a one-way ticket from San Francisco, USA, to Thessaloniki, Greece.

And just like that, my flirtation with slow travel turned into a date.

* * *

The Why

My most recent urge to travel to the states of Oaxaca and Chiapas in Mexico was to answer a call from my inner eco-artist to live in places entwined with a strong traditional and indigenous eco-art culture.

Elizabeth Gilbert, author of the famed book "Eat, Pray, Love," amidst a crumbling personal life followed her inner calling and took a life-changing journey of one and a half years to Italy, India, and Bali. She wanted to learn Italian in Italy and meditation in India. In Bali, she accidentally found love.

While in Mexico, I have met a few retired folks who want to start life over. They were slow traveling through Latin America on a trial run for a new place to call home. Some other travelers I encountered in Peru had spent months volunteering in an eco-village to immerse themselves in sustainability practices that they could then apply in their home country. A few were simply burnt out with their fast-paced careers and wanted to slow down enough to recover their inner stillness and natural rhythm—like I was.

Far from making this into a goal-setting venture, I am asking you to find your Why because having a purpose for your slow travel will give you *the motivation* to take the plunge in the first place. Later, it will propel you further on this earth-walk. In challenging times, it will be the fuel you will need to re-ignite the flame of wanderlust. On a practical level, the Why will help you plan your travels.

Above all, here is the most important reason for spending some time in getting clear on the Why. It is not *what* we do, but *why* we do it, that brings fulfillment to the what. So, spend some time to search for the Why and articulate it. Even if it is *"I want to escape the rat race, explore the world, and reconnect with myself,"* fair enough. Take a piece of paper and enunciate it.

You might ask: How do I find my Why?

Well, the only way to find it is to take a look inside yourself. Your specific life situation will give you your Why. What calls you? What is your heart longing for in a distant land? Is there something that you always wanted to learn?

 What is your Why?

The Where

If the Why of my trip is to explore the death rituals of ancient traditions, then I would start looking up the Day of the Dead in Mexico, the burning ghats of Varanasi in India, and the death ceremonies of Tibet. I would begin the flirtation with my visual appetite for pictures, reading about these rituals and the places, the stories, the mythology, and the spiritual beliefs underlying these rituals.

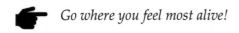 *The Why leads you to the Where.*

To decide the Where, the heart, the head, and the wallet have to coalesce in a healthy, vital play.

The heart

I could have picked many places to answer the call from my inner eco-artist to live where there is a long history of arts—Ethiopia, for one, and India could have been another. But I picked Oaxaca in Mexico.

Oaxaca has a long history of using natural materials like flowers, tree bark, fruits, insects to make natural pigments, all of which were fascinating and relevant for me. While this was a good enough reason to go to Oaxaca, it was not enough by itself. For as long as I could remember, I always *wanted* to go to Oaxaca. Perhaps because I found the name itself very intriguing and pronouncing it twisted my tongue? The thought of going to Oaxaca gave me goosebumps. The cells in my body began to vibrate with all the excitement of a kid who walks into a candy store and naturally gravitates toward the red heart-shaped gummy bears.

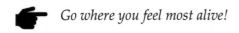 *Go where you feel most alive!*

Paul, another lifelong slow traveler who I met in Peru in 2018, considers the Where, as a soul calling.

> *"Part of my slow traveling is that it is my soul and or the Universe that picks my destinations, and it is always filled with 'soul contracts,' people I need to interact with for some time where I am of service to them, and from there, there is some sort of growth on both sides or at least an invitation to have something addressed as a part of that interaction."*

 *Follow that lead.*

The head

The head provides a reality check for the dream that is playing out in the heart.

Is it practical?

- *Can I secure a visa for more than X months with my passport?*
- *Is the country in a conflict/war zone?*
- *Is it relatively easy to connect with the local people despite the language barrier? Are there other expats living there?*
- *What is the availability of services that are important to me, such as a good Wi-Fi connection, vegetarian food, etc.?*

The wallet

I hate to break the news but the truth is that the wallet will have a significant say in deciding your Where.

Can I afford to travel where my heart desires to go and live there long-term on my budget?

We will dive more into this aspect in Chapter 4: Can I Afford It?

The How Long You Want Versus Can

John, the taco raconteur from Bainbridge Island, *"could stay out forever."*

I hear that!

But can we? There are practicalities in life that get in the way. The *want vs. can* dilemma is something where, again, the heart, the head, and the wallet have to collaborate with each other. You may not know exactly how long you want to go, but you need to have an approximate idea to get started. Ask yourself these questions:

- *What is my budget? How will I finance my travels?*
- *How long of a vacation can I secure? Can I work remotely? Can I take a sabbatical?*
- *How long of a visa can I get?* (For instance, even if I want to spend six to ten months in the Andalusian region of Spain, I cannot with my US passport. I am only allowed one three-month stay at a time.)

Available funds along with the cost of living and your lifestyle needs will put a cap on the How Long.

The How

Most slow travelers will take a flight to the first destination and then travel over land to others from there. Other slow travelers prefer to travel in an RV or a camper van. I have met others who have biked across the Americas and Asia, while others have gone even slower by cycling across Africa. A Canadian couple I once met in Peru kicked up the definition of slow travel another notch. They walked from southern India to northern India over six months to raise funds for a Canadian charity. Another Australian couple I met in Peru went sailing from the Americas to Europe over the Atlantic Ocean.

 What is your Where, How Long, and How?

The Conscious Slow Traveler

#1 Choose destinations that are contiguous.

By choosing destinations that are contiguous, you can travel from one to another by land, thereby reducing your carbon footprint. Let's say you pick Brazil, Peru, and Bolivia. You can then avoid flights and travel from one country to another by a bus/train combination. Being able to make short stops along the way to break the journey lends itself well to the ethos of slow travel.

#2 Slow travel is also a mindset.

Being able to get away for only a few days or a couple of weeks at a time due to work or other responsibilities doesn't mean you can't be a slow traveler. Slow travel does imply traveling over a longer period of time. Most slow travelers you encounter will be on a journey lasting a few months to a minimum. But the length of the journey by itself does not define slow travel. It is also a mindset.

- Choose to go to closer destinations instead of flying halfway around the world for just a couple of weeks.

- Choose only one destination for the entire duration when you have a short-break.

- On your next short-break go to the same destination *again* and forge a deeper connection each time.

Ilaria, my Italian belly dancing friend who I met in Milan during my time living and working there, cannot take long holidays due to work. This is what she does to satisfy the slow traveler in her:

"I love visiting new places, but once I've been there, I feel the need to go back a second time and a third time and I want to go back forever. So, I keep going back to the places I've already been. I want to melt with the atmosphere. I feel the need to be part of the places. I discover a new self in any place I go and it's like living multiple lives, one in every place and I need to go back because I need to keep those lives alive."

CHAPTER 4

CAN I AFFORD IT?

Contrary to popular belief, long-term slow travel *can* be cheaper than living your regular life at home. This book will show you the different ways in which you can save, but first let's tackle the primary concern that most aspiring slow travelers have:

Can I afford going on this date?

The first thing you have to decide is: How will you be funding your travel?

- You have saved up enough.
- You will be working while traveling.
- Retirement/pension/investment funds.
- Other sources.

Based on the answer, the second thing to decide is: What is your monthly budget?

Budgeting for long-term slow travel is not as hard as it looks. You can forecast *almost all* expenses before you even leave home. Once you have an approximate idea of what those could be for your destination, it will help you answer the question: *Can I afford going on this date?*

At this point, I encourage you to start a budget-expense spreadsheet with two sections: one-time expenses and recurring costs. The one-time expenses will include expenses such as the first flight out, travel insurance, visas, vaccinations, mailbox rental costs, etc. The recurring monthly costs, which will form the bulk of your travel expenditure, should include expenses such as apartment rent, utilities, food, local transportation, etc.

Keep plugging in these one-time and recurring costs in the spreadsheet as you continue reading this book.

Research Recurring Expenses

Your basic needs will remain the same, whether you are at home or traveling—accommodation, food, transportation, medical care, social life, etc.

Numbeo is very useful to arrive at an estimated cost of living in the country/city you want to travel to. This website provides a detailed breakdown of everyday expenses and the estimated cost of each. You can also make a cost-of-living comparison with another destination that you might be considering.

Rent takes the biggest bite out of the monthly budget. Even though Numbeo provides rent estimates, I also check Airbnb for rent prices in different neighborhoods for an accommodation that fits my needs. The monthly rental prices on Airbnb are, generally speaking, higher than if you were to get there and rent directly from a local person. But that works from a budgeting standpoint because I am already building some buffer into the rent estimate. I usually allocate 30% to 40% of my monthly budget towards rent. That still allows me to fulfill my lifestyle needs quite comfortably.

Plug these numbers into your budget-expense spreadsheet as steering numbers and add them up to arrive at the Total Base Expense.

Then add 15% to 20% to the Total Base Expense to account for local or seasonal fluctuations.

And If Budgets Aren't Your Forte...

I admit it. I am terrible at sticking to my budget. So, planning helps me stay close to, if not within my budget.

To account for my inability to stick to a budget, I give myself a buffer by adding 15% to 20% more to the Total Base Expense to arrive at the Final Estimated Monthly Expense.

Let's write this down mathematically to make it easier to understand.

Final Estimated Monthly Expense = Total Base Expense +
15% to 20% of the Total Base Expense to account for local
or seasonal fluctuations +
15% to 20% of the Total Base Expense as a buffer

Now that you have arrived at the final estimated expense, does that match your monthly budget? If not, then go back to the drawing board and see what you can adjust. Or go back to your Where and reconsider your destination choice.

Reserve Funds for the Unknown

Whatever my monthly budget may be, I always reserve a little extra for emergencies. As I wrote this chapter in San Cristobal de las Casas, Mexico, the COVID-19 pandemic brought the world to a standstill. Many travelers drew on their reserves and bought expensive one-way tickets to return home.

 Reserve some funds for these types of unknown and uncommon situations.

Keep Track of Travel Expenses

Apps like **TrailWallet** and **TrabeePocket** will help you keep track of your budget goals. After a couple of months, you will start noticing your spending trends. You can then readjust your spending or your budget if needed. **TripCoin** is another similar app, but with the added benefit of being available for use offline. So even if you are in a rainforest with no internet connection, you can still rely on it. **Spendee,** apart from being an expense tracker, also helps you plan your travels.

Budget First or Destination First?

If your destination is paramount, calculate the estimated cost of living where you intend to go. Can you afford it? If not, and there is no chance that you can compromise on your Where, you will have to find creative ways to make it happen. It will require you to do more research, adjust your lifestyle needs, do a work exchange, or reduce the amount of time you stay at that destination. It could be a little more time consuming to organize but certainly not impossible. So, don't give up.

If your budget is paramount, choose a destination where it will be enough to meet your lifestyle needs. Case in point, with a monthly budget of $1500, it is challenging to go on a long, slow travel to destinations known for a high cost of living such as Scandinavia or Japan. Unless you have friends there, have a scholarship of sorts, free accommodation lined up, cook many of your meals yourself, or do some part-time gig to supplement your budget, it's best to avoid countries that are notorious for having a high cost of living. However, the same budget will take you a long way in Latin America, Asia, and Africa.

In conclusion, which is more important to you: budget or destination?

For me, budget trumps destination and I manage other intentions around that.

Do a cost-of-living comparison in Numbeo to see how expensive it is to live in the different places you are considering. Add to this by an internet search for *"countries with a high cost of living"* and you will begin to get an idea of how expensive this date is going to be.

Currency Advantage

If you have flexibility in choosing your destination(s), then choose to go where your home currency will give you an advantage due to the exchange rate. Suppose that your home currency is Euro, and you travel to Mexico. At the time of writing this book, the exchange rate was 1 Euro to 24 *pesos*. This exchange rate will take you a long way in Mexico, whereas if you earn money in *pesos* and want to spend six months in Norway on a budget, well then, you'll have to find some creative ways to make your trip happen!

By traveling to cheaper destinations, you'll be able to get more bang for your buck, stretch your travel budget for longer, and explore more of our stunning planet.

My Sample Budget for One Year in Mexico

This is my budget allocation (in USD) for one year in Oaxaca and Chiapas in Mexico with a monthly budget of $1500. As you can see, I still have an extra $350 per month leftover that provides room for any unexpected expenses or for indulging myself every now and then. I also reserve additional funds for unforeseen situations and emergencies.

Item	Monthly allocation	Item	Monthly allocation
Private apartment	300	Language program	0
Groceries	200	Exploring the locale	75
Local transportation	25	Utilities	0
Dining out	100	Sports/Wellness/Exercise	50
Water	5	Clothing/Accessories	50
Medical care	50	Toiletries	25
Laundry	10	Art workshops	100
Drinks/Cafes/etc.	50	Miscellaneous	60
Social events	50	Monthly total	1150

Resources

	App	Website	Cost
Cost of living		numbeo.com	Free
Travel budget & expense management	TrailWallet (iPhone only)		Free basic version. Pay for more features.
	TrabeePocket		Free
	Spendee		Free basic version. Pay for more features.
	TripCoin (iPhone only)		Free

SECTION II

GOING ON A DATE

And if travel is like love, it is, in the end, mostly because it's a heightened state of awareness, in which we are mindful, receptive, undimmed by familiarity, and ready to be transformed. That is why the best trips, like the best love affairs, never really end.

Pico Iyer

CHAPTER 5

PLANNING THE NUTS & BOLTS

"I need to get visas for Greece, Turkey, Israel, and Egypt?" I grimaced.

My dream of spontaneously traveling overland through these countries for six months had ended with a resounding thud. To go on a date with the Mediterranean with my Indian passport, I needed to get all the visas ahead of time! The visa applications for each country required that I provide the date of entry, a physical address where I intended to stay, and produce proof of an arrival ticket.

I had none of these.

I only knew I was leaving San Francisco on April 1, 2002, for my first destination: Thessaloniki, Greece. At least I had that down! Then began the painstaking process of gathering paperwork for my visa applications.

I applied first for the Greek visa since I already had my ducks in a row for that one. Once I received that, I applied to the Turkish consulate with an approximate date of entry and the address of a hotel I found in the Lonely Planet guidebook. But without any proof of entry. Instead, I attached a copy of my flight ticket from San Francisco to Thessaloniki to the application form, pointed them to the Greek visa stamped on my passport, and wrote a letter.

"Dear Consul General of Turkey,

I plan to travel on a bus from Thessaloniki to Istanbul on <approximate date>, thus I am unable to provide you with proof of entry at this time..."

I crossed my fingers. They gave me a multiple entry visa.

I repeated the same for Israel. "…I plan to take a boat from Cyprus to Haifa…"

I crossed my fingers. They gave me a visa.

I repeated the same for Egypt. "…I plan to take a bus from Eilat to Dahab…"

I crossed my fingers and lo and behold, they issued me a visa.

P.S. In the end, I spent most of my six months living in Greece and Turkey. Israel ended up being a mere two-week sojourn. And Egypt to date still remains a mystery.

* * *

It's fine to flirt with an idea, but to take this flirtation out on a date requires a certain amount of research and planning. After all, you do want to make it an exhilarating and enriching experience, don't you? This is the point, however, when turning an idea into reality can feel daunting or overwhelming. There are so many details to iron out and things to take care of and plan, but don't let it demotivate you!

Just get started.

Begin by Researching Your Destination

In the late 90s and early 2000s, the Lonely Planet guidebooks were my bible for travel. Now, all the information is available in the digital form. Begin researching your travel destination at least three months before you plan to leave for things such as safety, accommodation, transportation, local markets, festivals, cultural events, travel advisories, etc.

Here are some of my most reliable and useful resources.

Local expat groups on Facebook

These have become my one-stop-shop for finding everything local and current related to my destination. When writing this chapter, I was in San Cristobal de las Casas, Mexico. I joined the San

Cristobal de las Casas Expat Community group on Facebook. It boasted a whopping 1,935 members, with new ones joining each day.

Some of these members have made San Cristobal de las Casas their home. Some are slow travelers, while some others are traveling through considering the possibility of buying property and settling there. Locals who are eager to meet other expats and travelers are also members of this Facebook group. It is a big market for them to advertise rental vacancies and other services.

Before I arrived at San Cristobal de las Casas, I was able to find a wealth of local information just by reading posts by other members or posting questions myself. I learned about the different neighborhoods, live music events, community activities, and approximate cost of renting an apartment.

 The most significant advantage is that the information is current and comes from people who are living there.

For this reason, I will refer to this group throughout the book as I find it to be the most reliable for day-to-day life information.

If there is an expat group on Facebook where you are going, then join the group *before* you leave to help you with the planning. Simply search for *"expats <city/country>"* on Facebook. If there is one, it will show up.

Internet resources

There is no shortage of travel information available on the internet. It is a valuable resource for research that cannot be ignored, except that the amount of information available is mind-boggling. Sorting through it is a chore by itself. It's important to remember that the point of doing internet research is NOT to know everything possible about the destination but just enough to get started.

When searching, be as targeted and specific as possible to reduce the information overload. For instance, search for "consulate of Benin in New York" instead of "how to get visas for Benin." Throughout this book and where relevant, I will provide you with pointed search phrases that you can use for your research.

Limiting the number of websites to read about the destination is another way to reduce the overwhelm. Identify not more than two to three websites that you like, bookmark them, and refer to them as and when you need. I like using **TripSavvy** for destination-specific information and **Tripadvisor** and **Yelp** for reviews on restaurants, hotels, spa services, tours, etc.

Travel guidebooks and online travel forums

Instead of buying paper guidebooks and making your bags heavy, you can purchase digital versions of well-known travel guidebooks such as **Fodors**, **Frommers**, and **Lonely Planet** directly from their website or **Amazon**. If you search for *"Travel guidebooks <destination name>"* on Amazon, you will find a ton of other guidebooks written by independent travelers as well.

Libraries also offer a selection of eBooks on travel destinations. Check your local library if they have an online service to borrow books from.

I will admit that I have a personal bias for Lonely Planet guidebooks because they bring up fond memories of the times when I began my global travels and they were my North Star. I continue to remain loyal to them when I wish to get a guidebook.

The **Lonely Planet Thorn Tree** online forum is another excellent resource for travelers to ask questions and share experiences, but the responses may come from people who are no longer at the place you are inquiring about. So, the information could be old. Nevertheless, I still rate this to be a valuable forum, and it's free to join. I always learn something useful in this forum.

The Consulate

Always revert to your destination country's consulate for official information such as travel advisories, visa and vaccination requirements.

Making Sense of Visas

Most of us will travel to countries on a visitor/tourist visa. These are the most straightforward and uncomplicated to obtain. Each country has its own unique visa requirements. Some will allow you to simply show up and stay, while others will require you to get a visa ahead of time.

Do you need one?

The answer depends on: What passport do you carry and where are you traveling to?

The best and most reliable way to research visa requirements is to check with your destination country's consulate.

When investigating visas, determine:

- Whether or not you can stay for the time duration you want to or longer on a visitor/tourist visa.

- Whether or not you can get a visa extension without leaving the country if you fall in love with the place and decide you want to stay longer. In some countries (e.g., Indonesia), this is possible using an agent.

- Whether or not you will have to leave the country after X months and return after Y days/months to get a new visa if you decide to extend your stay.

- Whether or not you are traveling to countries that are in a conflicted region. This might put the brakes on your travel plans and make you reconsider your destinations. Case in point, if you have traveled to Iran, then Israel will deny you an entry visa and vice versa.

 Start investigating the visa requirements at least three months in advance to account for processing time.

Will you need to register at the local immigration authority?

While researching visas, inquire about whether or not the foreign country requires you to register at the local immigration authority once you land there. For example, suppose you plan to stay in Mongolia for more than thirty days. In that case, it is required that you register with the local immigration authority within seven days of your arrival.

Travel Vaccinations

Whether you like it or not, some countries have mandatory vaccination requirements and you will not have a choice but to get them before you enter the country. For example, Tanzania requires proof of a yellow fever vaccination before setting foot in their country. Whereas, other vaccinations are only recommended.

What are the mandatory and recommended vaccination requirements for the country you are traveling to? Check with **CDC, WHO,** or country-specific consulates for information.

Cheaper alternatives for recommended vaccinations

Compared to many countries, travel-related vaccinations in the USA are expensive if not covered by health insurance. As an example, a yellow fever vaccination in the USA can cost anything from $150 to $350. In contrast, it will cost you between $0 and $10 paid out of pocket without any insurance in Peru.

I tend to avoid recommended vaccinations and let my natural immune system deal with it. If you decide to get the recommended vaccinations, then:

- Check if your health insurance covers them. If not, I recommend you wait until you get to your destination, locate a reputable clinic, and get them there. It will save you money.
- If you are not from the USA, compare prices with what they will cost you in your home country versus your destination country and then decide.

Get a vaccination card

Whenever you get a vaccination, ask the clinic/doctor to fill out your vaccination card stating the vaccination name, the date administered, and the validity. If you don't have a vaccination card yet, make sure to ask for one when you go in for your next vaccination. Some countries want to see this upon arrival.

Ensure you get all the vaccinations you intend to have at least a month before you travel to factor in time for it to start working before you leave and in case more than one dose is required.

Health Insurance Considerations

How does health insurance work in your home country? Here are a few things to check and decide:

- Can you pause your current health insurance while away instead of making expensive monthly payments?
- Can you change your plan to a cheaper option while you are away?
- Can you completely stop your health insurance before leaving and cross that bridge when you return?

International travel health insurance

Most countries in the world, barring the USA, have an affordable health care system even if you are paying out of pocket. Every time I go to India, I make sure to get a full medical check-up done. While I end up paying out of pocket for this, it is still much cheaper and easier than getting the equivalent done in the USA.

Some countries like Thailand, India, and Mexico have become hotspots for medical tourism. They offer state-of-the-art medical facilities and treatments at a fraction of the cost in the USA. Even without health insurance and paying all the travel costs out of pocket, they are still affordable. Simply do an internet search for *"medical tourism <country name>"* and you will get a ton of information on medical tourism possibilities for the country you plan to travel to. Why not take care of medical issues while slow traveling?

My credit card provides emergency medical and dental, emergency evacuation, and repatriation benefits. For the rest, I prefer to pay it myself. For these reasons, I have never purchased international travel health insurance. Many travelers feel safer combining expenses paid out of pocket for everyday health care expenses with international travel health insurance for big-ticket and ongoing health concerns.

Before you purchase any health insurance package, be sure to read the fine print and ascertain the following:

- Will you have to pay upfront, submit all the receipts, and then get reimbursed? Or can the insurance provider make payments directly to the medical care facility?
- Does your credit card cover some medical expenditures like hospitalization or an emergency? If yes, then don't pay for it again in the international travel health insurance you purchase.
- Carefully check what's covered and what's not, the deductible, and the maximum coverage amount. If you have an existing health issue, is that covered?

World Nomads and **Truetraveller** are recommended for long-term travelers. They also let you buy insurance while on the road, a notable advantage if you didn't purchase before leaving. Other more traditional travel insurance providers are **HealthCare International**, **Cigna**, **Allianz**, and **Aetna**.

Driver's License

What you *don't* want is for your driver's license to expire while you are on the road. If it is expiring close to the beginning of your trip and online renewal while on the road is not feasible, get it renewed before leaving.

If you intend to rent or buy a car in your destination country, remember to check whether your home country driver's license will be accepted there. If not, then plan to get an international driver's license in advance.

Smartphones

If you don't have a smartphone yet, I highly recommend you buy one. Smartphones with apps are useful on the road not just for information, navigation, and planning but also to keep in touch with friends and family around the world and for safety. There is no need to use those calling cards with long codes or using external devices like a magicJack for making international calls anymore.

Get your phone unlocked before you leave

Are you wondering what this means? Here is what it means:

Most of us buy a smartphone on a contract since these deals are very attractively priced. Here is a recent advertisement from T-Mobile.

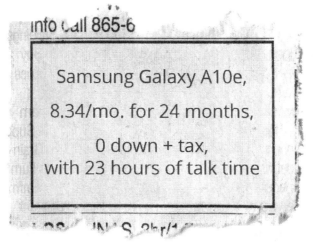

info call 865-6

Samsung Galaxy A10e,

8.34/mo. for 24 months,

0 down + tax,
with 23 hours of talk time

This translates to:

You will not be able to use this phone with any other provider other than T-mobile—in your home country or overseas—for twenty-four months.

This phone will be *locked* to T-Mobile for twenty-four months.

Phones purchased with these types of contracts remain locked even after the contract is over. This locking is detrimental to slow travel. Why?

 If your phone is locked, you will be unable to use a local SIM card in your destination country.

If you were taking a short holiday abroad, this wouldn't be an issue. But as slow travelers, we tend to live in a country for several months. We need to make local phone calls without having to pay expensive roaming fees. To do that, you *must* have an unlocked phone with you.

How can I get my phone unlocked?

There are two ways to get a phone ready for your travels:

#1 Call your provider *before* you leave and ask them to unlock your phone. Keep in mind that the new cellular provider in your destination country will *not* be able to help you. You must contact your provider at home since they'll be the only ones who'll be able to do it. If your contract is not yet over, you will have to pay off the phone's balance cost before your provider agrees to unlock your phone.

#2 Don't buy a phone on a contract. Pay the full cost upfront and verify that the phone is unlocked with the cellular provider or the store you bought it from.

That is all you will need to take care of as far as your phone is concerned before leaving for your trip. I will go into more detail on local SIM cards in Chapter 22: Stay Connected!

Become Digitally Savvy

Sometimes, I dream of going back to the days when I used to travel with a paper Lonely Planet guidebook. If you feel similarly inclined, take a chance, land in a new place, and navigate with the help of a guidebook. Otherwise, I recommend becoming digitally savvy. Having a smartphone with a few snazzy apps will help make your travel trails easy and relaxing.

Throughout this book, you will find recommendations for apps and websites that other slow travelers or I have found useful in the **Resources** section. In all likelihood, you will discover new apps or websites as you move along on your travels that you find helpful. Make a note of them and be sure to pass them onto other slow travelers and me. If you have not yet downloaded your *free* Slow Travel Planning Notebook, then do it now for a consolidated list of all the resources from this book. Stay in touch with me to receive periodic updates as I discover new or better ones.

The Conscious Slow Traveler

#1 Give back to the travel community.

A rule of thumb on the slow travel track is to give back when you can. During your research phase and after you have lived in your new destination, you will have picked up an invaluable amount of local know-how. Just as you found information that made your travel planning and eventually living there smoother, remember to give back by replying to questions posted by others on online forums and the local expat group on Facebook.

Offer information, initiate community activities, and engage in a healthy exchange. That's how the world of slow travelers goes around. Give back to the travel community.

Resources

	App	Website	Cost
Destination research	Tripadvisor	tripsavvy.com tripadvisor.com yelp.com	Free
Traditional travel guidebooks	Guides by Lonely Planet	lonelyplanet.com fodors.com frommers.com	Purchase the guide-books (digital or paper)
Travel insurance	Cigna Allianz Aetna Health	worldnomads.com truetraveller.com (for EU residents only) healthcareinternational.com cigna.com allianz.com aetna.com	Monthly or one-time payments
Travel vaccinations	CDC WHO Info	cdc.gov who.int	Free

CHAPTER 6

UNPLUGGING LIFE AT HOME

AUGUST 2018 - PISAC, PERU

"Bad news. We have to vacate our storage space by the end of November. Our landlord wants to convert the garage into a one-bedroom apartment," read a rare email from Jim, my long-term storage space mate in San Francisco.

"Oh, no!" I replied, disheartened, "I don't want to return to the USA right now."

I had just set up a studio space in my little casita on the slopes of *Apu Linli**, in the middle of a peach and apple orchard where I intended to spend the next few months painting. It was spring-time and the orchards were blooming with delicate pink and white flowers.

Jim and I had been sharing a huge garage converted into a storage space on Geary St., San Francisco, since 2009. I used a 8x10 wall space while Jim occupied the rest of it for an assorted collection of bikes, bicycles, and random things he found on the streets of San Francisco. Jim was a hoarder. According to him, these could be useful in the future.

"Could you at least leave a clear path for me to get to my stuff??" I would complain each time I entered our garage space to find it even more cluttered than before.

"Don't give me grief," he would retort in return.

I wondered what Jim was going to do with his collection now?

---

* *Apu Linli*, spirit of the sacred mountain Linli in the Andes of Peru

NOVEMBER 2018 - PISAC, PERU

I was experiencing a creative surge in my painting process with a potential exhibition in Cusco lurking around the corner. But I could no longer postpone my decision on how to handle this storage issue. Another friend, Scott, recommended a storage space in Novato, California.

"It's not fancy. I would call it the nickel and dime of storage spaces. But it's clean and secure. I've been using it for a few months now, and I haven't had any problems," he wrote.

After several tries, I succeeded in speaking to the manager over the phone and signed up for a month-to-month rental on an 8.5x10.5 storage unit.

"I have a truck. There's no reason for you to rush from Peru just to move your things." Scott offered to move my stuff from Geary St. to the unit in Novato for a very reasonable cost.

I was willing to consider all options to avoid returning to San Francisco.

FEBRUARY 2019 - NOVATO, CALIFORNIA

I opened the door to my new storage unit on a brief visit back to California. An unexpected sight greeted me. Boxes were thrown around helter-skelter, some upside down, some with the lid open and things spilling onto the floor. Two rats squealed at the light streaming through the opened door and scuttled out. The unit was wet due to rain and stunk from the combination of rat feces and mold!

I screamed.

"You new? Yeah, this place has had water leakage and rat problems in the past. The management knows but won't do anything about it." The guy from a few doors down empathized with me. He helped me drive out the remaining rats hiding behind the corner boxes in the dark.

"I'm sorry to hear that. Here, put this rat poison at the door," Ella, the manager, offered. "And call Jake. A year ago, water leakage from the rains damaged his expensive electronic equipment. He was initiating a lawsuit against the storage space. Maybe you two can team up together to collect damages." She handed me a piece of paper with Jake's number scribbled on it.

"Oh, really? Dunno what to say..." Scott shrugged his shoulders nonchalantly and went back to playing his guitar on the porch outside Whole Foods in Mill Valley.

Bottom line? I had to find a new storage place, pronto.

Lesson learned? Definitely.

* * *

Unplugging life at home is an emotional roller coaster ride filled with the excitement of a new adventure, the adrenaline rush of meeting the unknown mixed with the sadness of saying farewell, packing up, and leaving known people and places. Since slow travel most often than not involves going away for months at a time, you may have several things to take care of on the home front.

Packing Up Home

This process of packing up the home is a sentimental trip down nostalgia. It might reopen warm memories or defining moments from your life. It is also the time to purge what doesn't serve you anymore in this new phase of your life.

 In other words, it is a process of downshifting to simplicity.

Whether you are renting or are a homeowner, there are many decisions to be made. I recommend you start the process at least three months in advance and more if you have more important decisions to make, like selling your house.

What will you do with your home while you are away?

Here are some options:

#1 Rent it as a short-term rental and earn an income while on the road.

It is easier than ever before to rent out your home with online rental portals like **Airbnb**, **VRBO,** and **VacationHomeRentals**.

You can either self-manage the bookings and hire someone to look after the maintenance and the check-in/checkout process. Or go completely hands-free by letting a professional short-term rental management company handle everything for a percentage of the income.

#2 Rent it as a long-term rental and earn an income while on the road.

The traditional option is to give it over to a lease management company. They will rent out your home on a long-term lease and look after the day-to-day maintenance for a percentage of the rent. This way, you can go scot-free, look at the accounts every month and enjoy your slow travel life. Search on the internet for *"lease management companies <city/county name>"* to get started.

Long-term rentals are easier to self-manage while on the road since the turnaround is low. Post an ad on **Craigslist**, **Facebook Marketplace,** or **country-specific rental portals** (more on these resources in Chapter10: Accommodation) to find long-term renters. The best option, however, is to find someone through word-of-mouth. Far more secure, and you can feel more at ease knowing that your home will be looked after, while you are away.

You might not earn as much income with this option as with short-term rentals. But you will be able to cover your expenses (mortgage/rent, property taxes, etc.). Long term leases are also better from a maintenance and accounting perspective. Have a list of reliable and known handymen available, work out the maintenance with the renters, and enjoy your slow travel life.

#3 Exchange your home for another.

Let's say you want to spend six months in Greece and someone in Greece wants to spend six months in your hometown. **HomeExchange** connects people wishing to exchange their homes in different parts of the world. Read more about this in Chapter10: Accommodation.

#4 Lock it up.

If you are not worried about mortgage payments or the rent and feel unsure about renting out your home to another person, especially a stranger, then lock it up. If you do this, ensure that someone will go over regularly to check the property and collect your mail. Houses/apartments that are closed for long periods are attractive bait for theft. Installing a sound security/locking system will give you an added sense of security.

#5 Sell your home and clear the clutter.

Are you at a phase in life where you are looking for a fresh start? A new beginning? You want to create new memories in life without the attachments of the old. Or you may want to take the money and go traveling looking to set up a new home elsewhere in the world.

Then sell your home, clear out the clutter, and keep what is important and meaningful in a storage space until you want to put down roots again. If you return to your home country after a while, you will be a changed person. The decisions the "new you" will make with regards to a home will be quite different than what the "old you" would have made.

#6 End the rental lease and let it go.

If you are a renter, I think this is the best option. Keep your essential belongings in storage and let the rental go. Managing it from abroad is not worth the headache. You might be able to recover your rent but then you take up the administration and maintenance hassles. The only reason I would consider keeping a rental would be if it were for a rent-controlled apartment (e.g., in San Francisco) that I know I will not be able to get if and when I return.

#7 Become a minimalist.

I recently met Jason, a minimalist by design from the USA in San Cristobal de las Casas. He had let go of _everything_ at home—his house, car, and all his belongings. His only possessions were the contents of his small daypack. Yes, you read that right. _Only_ a daypack! Jason is intentionally experimenting with minimalism by living _only_ with a daypack.

Becoming an extreme minimalist like Jason requires a high level of detachment and desire for simplicity. It may not be for everyone. But if you desire to simplify your life, then begin by practicing a limited version. Simplify by letting-go of significant commitments like your house and car. Reduce your belongings down to fit in the smallest commercial storage space available.

Packing away things

Pictures, scrapbooks, that rocking chair you inherited from your grandmother, the king-size bed, camping gear, the coffee grinder your ex-boyfriend had gifted you, old CDs, books ...

What should you keep, and what should you let go? Packing up is nothing less than an exercise of inner feng-shui. Clear the clutter! Keep what is of sentimental value and let go of the rest.

Instead of throwing away your stuff, here are some ideas to put them to use.

- Organize a garage sale.
- Donate your things to a charity.
- Leave your stuff at a consignment shop. If it gets sold while you are gone, you will earn a percentage.
- Loan some things to friends, family, neighbors to use while you are away.
- Give them away!

Storage Space Considerations

Unlike Jason, if you decide to keep some of your belongings, you will need a place to store them, whether it be a commercial one or unused space in a friend's garage.

When looking for commercial storage space, don't be penny-wise and pound-foolish by choosing the cheapest option and compromising on quality. Once the pricing, location, and unit size works out:

- Visit the place to see an empty unit in person.
- Ask questions about water leakage/waterproofing, rat issues, and climate control.

- If the storage space is on the upper level, is there an eleva-tor? Think about climbing stairs to the second floor with all those heavy boxes.

- Is there 24/7 access, seven days a week? Will you have your access codes/keys, or will you be dependent on the office manager to open the gates for you?

If you are not in town and need to make a decision, like I was, pay a little more at a well-known storage space until you return. Then hunt for cheaper options. A quick internet search for *"storage spaces <city name>"* will give you several local options.

How to Handle Postal Mail

I dream of a time when I won't need to receive anything with postal mail. But alas, this is not a reality. At the very least, you will need to possibly receive renewed credit cards, driver's license, tax papers, and some critical bank documents by post. Unless you have decided to completely pack up your life in your home coun-try and end all ties, you will need an address for essential postal mail.

Friends and family

Do you have a friend or a family member who is willing to receive, sort, scan, discard, repackage, and forward your postal mail or other packages regularly to you?

Paid commercial mail forwarding services

The most obvious solution is to rent a PO Box from the local post office or other mailbox services. The problem with having a PO Box is that it's not a physical street address. Some places do not accept a PO Box as a valid address and having a street address is mandated. For instance, a driver's license requires a real street address. The other disadvantage is that they may not forward your mail internationally. That means you will have to wait until you return to collect all your posts.

Since 2017, I have been using the services of **Traveling Mailbox** (available only in the USA). They provide a real street address where I can safely receive my important postal mail and other packages. I can manage and control all aspects of my mail from an online dashboard.

Other similar services are **Anytime Mailbox, iPostal1,** and **Post Scan Mail**. These are also available outside of the USA.

 What mailbox options are available in your country?

Can the renters/lease management receive your mail?

If you have decided to rent out your home while away, check if the renters or the lease management company will collect your postal mail and post it to you from time to time.

 Forget-me-not!

File a change of address before you leave.

 What other things do you need to consider while packing up home that are unique to you? Pets? Car? Boat?

Resources

	App	Website	Cost
Rental options	Airbnb Vrbo Vacation Rentals HomeExchange	airbnb.com vrbo.com vacationhomerentals.com homeexchange.com	Service fee on rentals.
	Facebook	facebook.com craigslist.org	Free
Mailbox services	Traveling Mailbox Anytime Mailbox Renter iPostal1 PostScan Mail	travelingmailbox.com anytimemailbox.com ipostal1.com postscanmail.com	Monthly/ yearly subscription.

Chapter 7

Money Matters

May 2012 - Kuala Lumpur, Malaysia

It was 8 p.m. My colleagues had left a few minutes ago. While packing up my bag to leave for the day, I noticed that I did not have enough Malaysian *ringgits* for a taxi to my apartment in Gardens Court. I made a mental note to myself—withdraw cash at the mall on the ground level of the Petronas Twin Towers before getting into a taxi. I hopped out of the elevator and made my way to the usual ATM I got cash from.

Only this time, the ATM declined the transaction.

Hmmm. Maybe the machine is low on cash. Let me try a smaller amount. Once again, I tried with my USA Visa card. The same result.

This is strange. Why is it declining the transaction? I was puzzled. I tried a different ATM speculating that this one must be out of cash. But once again, I got the same result.

Next, I tried my Danish Mastercard ATM card. It was declined as well. Now I was getting worried. Why were both the cards I used most often not working? Moreover, how was I to return to my apartment with no cash? In 2012, the taxis in Kuala Lumpur did not accept credit cards. There was no other way to return to my apartment other than walking the seven km.

The last ATM card I had with me was my Indian Visa cash card, which I rarely used. I was not at all sure if it was set up to dispense cash internationally. But I had nothing left to lose. So, I tried and hallelujah! It worked! Filled with relief, I took the money and jumped into the first taxi waiting outside the mall entrance. My brain was furiously working out all the plausible reasons why my cards were not working.

As soon as I reached my apartment, I dialed my US bank's toll-free 24/7 customer support number using Skype.

"We are sorry for the inconvenience, Ms. Gesota. But your card has been blocked," explained the banker calmly.

"BLOCKED?" I wanted to yell, but instead, I asked calmly, "Why?"

"Our system has detected suspicious activity."

"What suspicious activity?" I was baffled.

"The system has detected withdrawals using your card in Kuala Lumpur and Bali."

"That's right. I am in Kuala Lumpur, and I was in Bali last weekend. I have been using my card here for a couple of months."

"Ok, Ms. Gesota. In that case, can you verify these transactions?"

"Of course!" I logged into my bank account. All the transactions were indeed mine.

"Thank you, Ms. Gesota. We can now lift the block on your card, and it should be available immediately."

I heaved a sigh of relief.

"So that was it? Because your system detected withdrawals in Kuala Lumpur and Bali, you blocked my card? I could have been stuck in a bad situation with no cash! You could've at least sent me a warning email that you were planning to block my card!" I almost screamed at him.

"We are sorry, Ms. Gesota. But this is automated in the system."

"But I am overseas right now and I won't be returning to the USA anytime soon. I need to use my card to make withdrawals. Does that mean after every few transactions, your system will block my card? And I must keep calling you to unblock it?"

I couldn't believe this!

"No, Ms. Gesota. If you are going to be abroad for a while, you need to inform us so we can set that in our system. That will stop the system from triggering a block on your card. Would you like me to set that up for you?"

I was relieved to know that there was a solution.

"Yes, please. Thank you."

I then dialed the customer support for my Danish bank using Skype. It turned out that my Danish card was blocked because I had exceeded my card's monthly withdrawal limit! It was quite simple to take care of as well. The banker upgraded my account, which would give me a higher monthly withdrawal limit.

Lessons learned about banking while on the road? Absolutely.

* * *

While most of the payments and day-to-day spending in the USA happen with cards, a large part of the world still operates with cash. The more off the beaten path you go, the more you will need hard cash in hand. Moreover, paying in cash will get you lower prices in many places.

To keep things simple:

- Don't withdraw cash using credit cards to avoid low exchange rates, high transaction fees, and increasing the risk of fraud.
- Reserve credit cards for high-ticket payments like flights, hotels, car rental agencies, etc. Pay the local guide, the street vendors, the vendors at the farmer's market, the handicraft market, etc. in cash.
- Don't get the foreign exchange from the departing country. As soon as you land in the new country, head straight to the ATM, and get enough cash to last a few days.

Ways to Exchange Money on the Road

ATMs

ATM withdrawals overseas are my preferred way to get cash in the local currency. Here is why:

- I consistently get the best exchange rate while using an ATM.
- ATMs have skyrocketed across the world, making it easy to

get cash in hand whenever I want, regardless of holidays or official business hours.

- If my card gets stolen or lost, I can cancel it anytime by calling my bank. The effect is immediate. Some banks even provide expedited service to ship the new card to you anywhere in the world.

- Many banks provide an emergency cash advance via wire transfer at the closest Western Union or a partner location in case of an ATM card theft or loss.

Prepaid debit cards

Prepaid debit cards have become popular among travelers. These can double up as a credit card, but the difference with regular credit cards is that they are prepaid. That means you can use these as a debit or a credit card only when there is money in the account.

The most significant advantage I see of using these prepaid debit cards is that you decouple your primary financial account from the one you use while on the road. That directly reduces the risk of fraud with your primary financial account. If there is fraud with the account linked to the prepaid debit card, your loss will be minimal since you will only have the operating amount of cash in it.

Check out the prepaid **Simple Visa** debit card. Simply transfer the amount of money you want to spend during your travels and start using it. The card is chip-enabled, works internationally, comes with a budgeting tool to help you plan, and you can set up online payments for recurring bills as well. **Revolut** is another card that is popular among travelers.

Money exchange services

I don't recommend using money exchange services like Forex or Travelex as they give a reduced exchange rate and charge transaction fees. The hit can be as much as a 15% loss. The same applies to local banks. Not to mention the long lines, slow service, and you have to adhere to the bank's business hours. I use them only in an emergency to exchange my stash of hard USD/Euro notes.

Traveler's checks

Before ATMs skyrocketed, traveler checks were a popular way to get cash while traveling. The most significant advantage being that, unlike cash, if stolen, they can be replaced.

But the disadvantages far outweigh the advantages.

- Cashing a traveler's check requires locating a partner bank or a currency exchange agent where you can cash them. Which means you need to adhere to their working hours. If you run out of cash on a Sunday or a series of holidays, you are out of luck.

- You may have to settle for a lower exchange rate.

- Issuing banks charge fees to issue the traveler's checks. Plus, you might be charged processing fees at the other end while cashing them.

- If they get stolen, the process of replacing them is cumbersome. You have to submit all the unused serial numbers with the original receipts to the issuer to get the replacements. Depending on where you are in the world and where your issuer's nearest partner location is, you might have to wait for anything between a day and several days to get the replacements.

ATM/Debit/Credit Cards

The rule of thumb is to take three cards with you.

#1 One credit/debit card

#2 One ATM card

#3 One backup ATM card. In case one gets lost, demagnetized, 'swallowed' by an ATM, stolen, or simply stops working, then you have another one to rely on.

Don't take more cards with you. The more you carry, the more you have to keep track of them and worry about fraud, card theft, or losing them.

VISA and Mastercard will work everywhere where cards are

accepted. Discover and American Express are not accepted universally. To be on the safe side, make sure that you carry a VISA/Mastercard card with you. I take one of each to make sure I am covered no matter where I am in the world.

7 Things to Take Care of Before Hitting the Road

#1 Apply for cards with an international bank.

Banks like Citibank or HSBC have physical branches and partner banks in many countries where you can withdraw money without any foreign transaction fees.

#2 Find cards with zero international transaction fees.

If you plan on getting new cards, then apply for ones that have no foreign transaction fees. **CreditCards** provides accurate and reliable information on different credit cards and what they cover.

#3 Will your cards expire while you are on the road?

If yes, check with your bank before you leave on handling card renewals while on the road. Can they post you the new cards where you will be? If not, request to get them renewed before you leave. My bank will not ship my new cards to any location other than the official address on their records. But since I use the address given to me by the Traveling Mailbox service, they forward me all my mail internationally, including renewed credit cards.

#4 Stick to a 4-digit ATM PIN.

Back in 2003, I was out of luck in Chichicastenango, Guatemala. That little village had only one ATM, which did not accept my 6-digit ATM card PIN. Since it was a Sunday, the bank was closed. I had $1 in my pocket. Luckily, a couple of Australian backpackers rescued me from having to sleep outside the Santo Tomas church, cold and hungry. They loaned me $10, which was enough to cover my hotel and food for the night, and a bus to Lake Atitlan the following day.

A 4-digit ATM PIN is the norm around the world. Anything other than a 4-digit PIN might leave you stranded somewhere with no ability to withdraw cash.

#5 Travel with chip-enabled cards.

Cards with a magnetic strip are on their way out. If your card is not chip-enabled, check with your bank if it can issue you one. Chip-enabled cards are also less susceptible to fraud.

#6 Is your monthly ATM withdrawal limit going to suffice for your monthly expenses?

If not, check with your bank to increase the monthly withdrawal limit to match how much you will need.

#7 Does your credit card cover rental car insurance?

If so, you will be able to save huge amounts of money by not buying collision damage insurance from the rental car company. It's quite common when renting a car that the rental price itself is cheap. It's the added cost of collision damage insurance that jacks up the price. If you intend to rent a car on your travel and your existing card does not cover rental car insurance, I recommend that you apply for a new credit card that does. Again, **CreditCards** is useful for finding which cards include this insurance.

Handling Fraud Alerts

Banks have systemized checks to detect fraudulent usage of your card. One of them is your card being used internationally and from unusual locations. If the system detects a few such withdrawals, it will put a temporary block on your card. While this is an imperative measure to protect your card from fraud, you could get stuck somewhere not being able to withdraw cash when you need it—like I was in Kuala Lumpur.

Before leaving on your trip, call your bank and inform them that you will be traveling for a while and using your card in different countries. Ask them what options are available and how to handle your card not getting blocked. Then make an informed decision.

You may have to choose between these two options:

   #1 Keep the fraud alert and risk your card getting blocked while you are on the road.

#2 Take your card *off* the fraud alert. This could be risky but will not leave you stranded for money.

I have chosen the second option but diligently check my card's transaction history from time to time.

Set Up Online Banking & Bill Pay

Do you bank online? If not, then it is time to get it set up before you leave for your trip.

You can then check your account online and download relevant documents like tax papers from anywhere in the world—albeit on a secure internet connection. Setting up automatic bill pay will free you from unwanted travel companions such as property taxes, utility bills, mailbox fees, insurance fees, etc.

Life on the road is much easier this way.

If online payments are not possible with your bank, start thinking about how you will take care of required payments back home, if any, while you are away.

Reminders and Notifications

It is *very* easy to forget and lose track of financial obligations back home, especially if you have been deep in a remote area for a month or two with little to no internet connection.

Electricity bill? Taxes? Insurance payments? Huh? What is that?

It helps when the phone beeps a gentle reminder well before the due date:

Remember to renew your phone subscription before mm/dd/yyyy.

I always set my reminders in advance of the deadline. That way, if I am in a place where the internet is scarce, unreliable, or unsecured, it gives me some time to get myself to a place where I can make a secure online financial transaction.

The last thing I want is to pay the penalty for late payments, have to make international calls and hang on with customer support for hours to sort out issues, or get my account hacked because I logged in on an unsecured internet network.

Resources

	App	Website	Cost
Credit cards		creditcards.com	Free
Prepaid debit cards	Simple-Mobile Banking Revolut	simple.com revolut.com	Free

CHAPTER 8

PACKING FOR THE TRIP

It was my farewell dinner. I had cooked an Indian-Mexican fusion meal, and Merle, my Airbnb host, had prepared his special margaritas. He had relished my cooking during the days I had stayed at his guesthouse and I had enjoyed his experiments with breakfasts. We had become instant lifelong friends. I was on my way to Oaxaca city, and Matt, another guest and slow traveler, was on his way to Chiapas.

"I can't believe that you carry Indian spices with you!" Merle gushed while making a fresh batch of margaritas.

"Yes, that's the one thing I *must* carry with me on my long travel trails. I love cooking! Not that I cook Indian food every day. But now and then, I need to appease my Indian taste buds. Plus, I can experiment with local food fused with Indian spices. Like I did today with the platano tacos. It is one of the ways I make a home away from home."

"No wonder your bags are so heavy," joked Matt.

"Ah, well! I have other things in there that make them heavy," I laughed.

"Joking apart, as a traveler myself, I completely understand that sentiment. For me, it's portable speakers," Matt continued.

"Seriously? How big are they?" Merle remarked while handing us the margaritas.

"Wait. Let me show you." Matt dashed off to his room and returned with a ten-inch-tall black speaker.

"Don't go by size. The sound quality is fantastic." He handed it to me like a child brandishing his favorite toy.

"It's heavy! How do you manage to take this on the plane?" I asked, weighing the speaker in my hand.

"I cut out other things. Listening to music is important for me while on the road, and I can't compromise the sound quality. They are to me, what your Indian spice box is for you."

Merle nodded his agreement. The three of us looked at each other in silence with a shared understanding of life on the road.

"Salud," we raised a toast to our travel stories and the setting sun on Merle's rooftop garden.

I knew that as long as Merle lived there, I would always have a place to stay in San Miguel de Allende.

* * *

What to pack? How much to pack? How to pack?

To answer these questions, you have to return to your Why, Where, How, and How Long.

What to Pack?

If your Why is to enroll in yoga courses for the next year, you will pack yoga clothing, yoga mat, meditation cushion, yoga books, etc.

If your Where includes places of higher altitudes and the beach, then your bags will have multipurpose cold weather and beachside clothing.

If you are traveling by RV or a camper van, you will have the luxury of taking your favorite pillow and that "Forever Young" cactus your sister gifted you that you cannot leave behind.

If you are like me, you may not know the exact How Long at the start of your trip, but you will have an approximate idea. Depending on whether you plan to be away for two months or two years, what you pack will vary. To give you an idea, if I were going away for a minimum of six months, my list of what I *cannot* live without would be longer, and I would pick up other necessities along the way.

The rule of thumb is to pack everything you will need, but stay minimal.

Pack light, travel smart

No matter what season or where you are going, for ultimate flexibility, the golden rule of travel is to pack in a way that you can dress in layers. That makes each item suitable for multiple weathers and multiple places—from high altitudes to beaches.

#1 Don't pack...

In 2017, I met Lisa. She was co-managing a guesthouse I was staying at in the Sacred Valley of the Incas, Peru. Her six-month visa was up, and she was packing to leave.

"Hey, do you want some shampoos or cosmetics by any chance?" She asked while I was lounging in the hammock on the porch, taking in the afternoon sun.

"I need to get rid of all my cosmetics, soaps, and shampoos that I brought with me from the USA to make space in my bag for all the souvenirs I bought here," she explained.

"How much do you have?" I queried, wondering how getting rid of a couple of bottles would help her make space in her bag?

"I have a suitcase full of them," she answered sheepishly.

"A suitcase full of them?" I stared at her.

"I brought two suitcases with me—one filled with cosmetics, shampoos, and soaps. I knew I wouldn't find the brands I use here in Peru," she admitted.

 Don't pack things you can buy locally and adapt to what is available.

While at it, leave out all the "just-in-case" items. If your destination is nowhere near the sea, don't pack snorkel gear just-in-case you go to a place known for beautiful coral reefs and tropical fish. Buy or rent the equipment if and when you get there.

#2 Pack like a minimalist.

Jason, the minimalist by design, was living out of the contents of his small daypack. This lifestyle could be a bit extreme for some of us. But if you are keen to pack like a minimalist, the way to ease into being one is through practice. One way is to store away all the things you think you want to take with you in a room or storage. Each day, pull out only one thing that you want to take with you. Do this for two weeks. At the end of two weeks, what you got is what you will travel with.

#3 Make a waterproof ID card.

Place one card in each of your bags and one in your carryon in a way that they are easily spotted. Once you have landed, keep one in your wallet or daypack when you are out and about.

Name: _____

Phone: _____

Email: _____

From: <country/city name> _____

Emergency contact: _____

#4 Small things come in very handy.

I always carry a small sewing kit, earplugs, a basic first aid kit, a couple of linen shopping bags, and a few mesh bags to hold small items like underwear, dirty laundry, or socks.

#5 Take the right power adaptors.

Don't forget to research the type of electrical wall socket used in the country you are going to (two flat prongs, two round prongs, three round prongs, two flat prongs and one round prong, etc.), or else you might be left with no way to charge your digital devices.

The electrical system of your destination country may be different than the one in your home country. If it is not compatible with your device chargers, then buy a power adaptor before leaving.

After purchasing numerous adaptors for each country that I traveled to during my green days as a slow traveler, I invested in a universal power adaptor that works in all countries.

REI provides a detailed guide to help you get sorted. Just search on the internet for *"REI electricity guide."*

#6 Carry proof of vaccinations you have had to date.

If you have taken the travel vaccinations, remember to pack your vaccination card.

#7 Keep your insurance details and credit card coverage benefits handy.

Such as the policy number, the number to call for reimbursements, and proof of coverage.

#8 Stash away some hard currency for emergencies.

No one anywhere in the world will refuse USD or Euro hard currency. I suggest keeping between 50 to 100 of either stashed away in a side pocket somewhere that you can retrieve during emergencies.

#9 What do you need to manage your dietary restrictions?

If you follow a particular diet, pack whatever you need to support it and stay healthy until you find a local source or order online. I have seen people with gluten intolerance carry digestive enzymes. These help them digest gluten when they have little choice but to eat gluten-based foods. Such as during long waits at bus stations.

#10 Pack your favorites that may not be available in the foreign country.

In 1999, during a work trip to Costa Rica, I met a fellow traveler who was carrying a few small packets of oatmeal with him. Surely, oatmeal is available everywhere, I thought? He didn't want to take any chances as he was planning to travel to remote areas. Oatmeal was his comfort breakfast food for those times when he longed for a taste of home.

Similar to him, I prefer to not take chances with a few things. Yellow *mung daal** is hard to find in Latin America, so I always carry a small pack with me for those times when I long for my *khichdi†*.

Pack in an attitude!

There are two types of travelers. The ones who leave their assumptions and expectations at home and those who don't. Be the one in the first category and pack:

- A beginner's mind
- Child-like curiosity
- Willingness to be challenged

All the more so if you have already been on the travel track before. As seasoned travelers, we tend to develop the mindset of "been there, done that." In doing so, we lock ourselves up into a box called "I know," leaving no room for the new and the spontaneous to pop its head in.

 Let us not be dimmed by familiarity.

What can I NOT live without?

This question becomes increasingly relevant when on the road for a longer time.

These are the things with which we make a home away from home and to dispel those gloomy days when they set in.

As you know from my anecdote in this chapter, at present, it is my box of Indian spices. For Matt, it is his portable speakers. For Emma, a slow bicycle traveler from Sweden, her little red iPod she bought in 2007 gives her an incredible feeling of happiness thinking about all the small and big journeys she had gone on since she first bought it.

Kriszta, who gave up her "shiny" management job, does not travel without her pillow in the form of a teddy bear head that her Mom gave her when she was nine years old. Tamara used

---

* *mung daal*, split and husked mung bean
† *khichdi*, comforting Indian dish traditionally made with lentils and rice

to sail or bicycle but decided that even that was too fast for her: *"Things were zooming by."* She now travels by walking and cannot live without pre-moistened individually wrapped facial masks while on the road.

Flight Limitations

Apart from the How of your travel plans, if you intend to take a flight to your first destination, the flight luggage limitations will put a cap on how much you can take with you. It will vary from airline to airline and whether you are flying international or domestic/inter-region.

 Verify the free check-in luggage weight limitations and extra baggage fees before you begin packing.

Even as a seasoned traveler, I have found myself with overweight suitcases and thrown out stuff at the airport because I ignored this point when packing. A few times, I have improvised by taking out a bunch of warm clothes from my check-in suitcase and wearing it all on board the flight. I got some odd looks on the plane. But it was either that or throw away things in the airport trash bins. I chose to let go of my vanity.

How to Pack?

Jurgen, a tech entrepreneur I met at an Agile project management workshop in Berlin, slow travels in his gypsy caravan—a BMW. A minimalist by nature, he organizes his suitcase into stacks: formal clothes, casual clothes, supplements and first aid, toiletries, underclothing, and so on. Each stack goes into a waterproof ziplock bag labeled with the contents, which he then neatly lays out into his suitcase.

"This way, I know exactly where everything is," he grinned, proudly showing me his art of packing in the Airbnb apartment we were sharing. He is always packed two days before he is going to leave.

"What if you have some things that don't fit into any of these categories?" I was a bit wary of his meticulous packing style.

"Then, I make a new one. How is that for OCD?" He gave me a sardonic smile.

In contrast to Jurgen, I suffer from CCD (Chaotic Compulsive Disorder). Don't look up that term. My pen just made it up! All jokes aside, my packing strategy is similar to Jurgen's, just not as meticulous. Categorizing and packing things into smaller bags is a slick way to organize and be able to actually *find stuff* when needed instead of rummaging through the entire bag just for those swimming goggles!

My other packing strategy is this:

> Bag #1: Pack everything that I will need as soon as I land until I find long-term accommodation.
>
> Bag #2: Everything else.

This way, I don't need to unpack Bag #2 until I have settled into a long-term place. This saves me the hassle of having to unpack and repack two bags.

Yes, I travel with two bags since I tend to be away for more extended periods—a minimum of six months. In recent years, I have begun to carry some essential art equipment with me, such as my paintbrushes.

Some travelers use vacuum storage bags to pack. These occupy less space, meaning you can squeeze in more stuff without increasing the weight of your suitcase—a significant advantage when flying.

My Packing List for a Trip to Peru

January–July 2017 - the Amazon jungle and Cusco, Peru

This trip was split between the heavy humidity and violent downpours of the Amazon jungle and the high altitude cold of Cusco. It meant packing for extreme climates. I was flying from San Francisco to Lima on an international flight and from Lima to Cusco on a domestic airline.

Long-sleeved loose shirts (3), tops (3)	Headlamp (1)	Thermos (1)	**What can I NOT live without?**
Long and loose baggy pants (3), jeans (1)	Natural mosquito repellents (two types)	Water bottle (1)	Basic paint-brush set
Sarongs (2)	DEET based mosquito repel-lent (as a backup)	Sunscreen	A journal, pens, and pencils
Hiking shoes (1)	Mosquito net (1)	Dr. Bronner's soap and shampoo	Paper for painting and sketching
Waterproof sandals (1)	Citronella essential oil for mosquitoes	Other toiletries	Acrylics primary colors
Long socks (3), short socks (2)	Mosquito repel-lent candles	Multivitamins	Incense, tarot cards, stones
Swimwear (1)	Humidity absor-bent pouches for electronics	Vitamin B12	Small altar items
Towel (1), Quick-drying towel (1)	Waterproof bags for electronics	Some jewelry	Bergamot, Lavender essential oil
Winter jacket (1)	Daypack (1)	iPhone, MacBook Pro	
Fleece hoodie (1)	Raincoat (1)	Canon digital camera	
Warm muffler (2)	Books (2)	Universal power adaptor (1)	
Warm leggings (2)	Yoga mat (1)	Earplugs (1)	

Dress (1), Long skirt (1), Short skirt (1)	Tea Tree essential oil	Chase United Credit card, ATM/debit cards (2)	
Warm woolen gloves (2), wool headband (2)	Toilet paper (1)	Malaria pills	
Shawl (1)	Small emergency sewing kit	Passport, driver's license	
Long-sleeved sweater and tops (3)	First aid kit	Vaccination card	
Underclothing	Mesh bags (2)		
Dress sandal (1)	Hat (1)		

Note: On this trip, I did not take my spice box with me. My "What can I NOT live without?" list was different at that time.

The "Comprehensive Packing Checklist" at the end of this book includes all the essentials and extras you may or may not need depending on your destination. It can come in handy when you're planning and want to be strict and minimal about what you put in your bags. Download and print it from the free "Slow Travel Planning Notebook" and keep checking off the list as you pack.

The Conscious Slow Traveler

#1 Make a green choice.

When shopping for your trip, buy eco-friendly products. For instance, buy a bamboo toothbrush instead of a plastic one, biodegradable soaps, shampoo, and toothpaste. The environment and your inner panda will thank you.

#2 Seek quality over quantity.

Quality products are more expensive but will last longer, which means less trash on planet Earth. I used my Ecco hiking boots for a good six years before someone stole them in Peru.

#3 Say NO to single-use plastic.

Pack an empty non-plastic water bottle in your carry-on to the airport and fill up with water from the drinking stations on the other side of security. Use this non-plastic bottle during your travels instead of buying plastic water bottles.

CHAPTER 9

ALL ABOUT FLIGHTS

Slow travelers bus, train, walk, bicycle. We cruise along the roads on bikes, in camper vans, or RVs. Some others cross the high seas in ferries or sailboats. In other words, we overland, i.e., travel over the land or the seas domestically, inter-region, or when crossing an international border to the next destination. We make stops along the way to inhale and exhale. We prefer not to fly in the skies.

However, there are times when taking a flight is necessary, such as kick-starting your slow travel trip with an international flight out to your first destination, or when overlanding is not a viable option. For instance, when going to Iquitos in Peru.

Iquitos, the gateway to the Peruvian Amazon jungle, is the largest town in the world not accessible by road. The only way to reach Iquitos is to fly or take a long winding boat trip down the Amazon River. I would highly recommend taking the boat trip, except that I have heard nasty stories from other travelers about pirates on this boat trip. Seriously! Until I have not verified the validity of these stories, I will fly to Iquitos. I recommend you do the same. Safety comes first.

There is nothing slow about flying but since it is necessary, let's do it on a budget. We will return to overlanding in Chapter 13: Overlanding & Getting Local.

Flying During COVID-19 Times

We all know that the airline and travel industry is going through many changes in the wake of COVID-19. When writing this book, countries have opened travel only within "travel bubbles," i.e., only between specific countries. Some flights are getting canceled.

Some airlines might even go bankrupt. It is crucial to keep COVID-19 induced uncertainty in mind when booking flights. While what I have written in this chapter still holds, it might change as the airline industry settles into a new normal. Look out for a new edition of this book or a free supplement when that happens.

Meanwhile, these are my two critical recommendations when booking flights.

#1 Search and compare flights through the travel discount websites but buy the flight from the airline's website directly, even if you have to pay a few extra dollars. In case of a flight cancelation, processing refunds or changes directly with the airline will be easier.

#2 If you find a good deal, check the cancelation and refund policy. Due to the uncertain times, ensure that if the flight is canceled or you have to change your plans due to COVID-19, you can get a full refund or at least a voucher for future use.

Compare Before Buying

I have consistently had a good experience with **Kayak**. Since no one travel discount website can give all the possible airlines and combinations, I also check **SkyScanner** and **Google Flights** to make a fare and route comparison. For domestic or regional flights, I also compare the discount travel website fare with the fare on the airline's website.

When making a fare comparison, compare apples to apples and oranges to oranges. This is how:

- **Compare the after-tax fare**

  Some websites list the ticket prices before tax. That might fool you into thinking you got a cheaper fare in comparison to another website that shows you the fare but after-tax!

- **Check the baggage check-in policy**

  Is checked-in baggage included in the price? How many pieces are you allowed to check-in for free? If you have to pay, how much would that be per piece? Is there a fee for carry-on luggage, or is it free? Beware of these hidden costs. Initially, a fare might look cheap, but it may no longer be the lowest after adding the baggage check-in fees.

- **Compare the transfer times**

    If the transfer time between two flights is less than one hour, that is somewhat risky for international flights. Is the layover too long with no reasonable option of stepping out of the airport? There may be a terminal change involved with baggage re-checking required with very little transfer time. Weigh in these factors before buying the cheapest flight. A few dollars saved here may not be worth it.

- **Compare in the same currency**

    When browsing for fares on different websites in different currencies, don't forget to convert them into one currency before comparing them.

Book Early, But Not Too Early

Once, I thought, what if I buy my ticket from San Francisco to Mumbai six months in advance? Maybe I will come across some dirt cheap fares. On the contrary, I found that the flights that far out were more expensive than when I had booked even one week in advance for that sector.

So, book early but not too early.

For domestic flights, start your search forty-seven days out on an average. And for international flights, about three months in advance.

 COVID-19 Times Warning:

Booking early may not be the wisest option due to the uncertainty of flights and country lockdowns. In these times, it might be better to book about three weeks before the date you want to fly.

Last-Minute Deals: To Wait or Not to Wait?

With the way online booking and airline pricing work, sometimes, last-minute deals can end up being cheaper than buying in advance. But I do not recommend this approach for your first international flight to kick-off your slow travel trails. You don't want to be in a situation where you have packed up your home, the renters are moving in, your stuff is in the storage space, your bags are packed, and you don't have a ticket in hand.

Because you are waiting for a last-minute deal!

Unless you have super flexibility, don't wait until the last minute. Use this option once you are on your slow travel trail, want to fly domestically or inter-region, and don't have a fixed date. Then wait for the last-minute deal to come around and jump on a plane.

Fly for Free

Sign-up for frequent flyer program

Become an airline frequent flyer member, if you are not already. Every time you fly with your airline or a partner airline, you will accumulate miles that you can redeem later for free flights.

I don't think I am going to be flying that much, so what's the point?

Trust me when I say that each mile counts. The time will come when you will start to get free flights. Not just that, you will also begin to get other perks such as complimentary airport lounge passes, free upgrades, priority boarding, free checked-in baggage, etc. As a slow traveler, the most significant advantage of having miles is flexibility. I have booked international flights at the last-minute using miles without worrying about high fares during peak seasons.

In the process, I have saved thousands of dollars. Plus, you have nothing to lose. These programs are *free* to join.

Before choosing your frequent flyer program, consider these points.

Choose an airline that is a member of one of the three major

airline alliances - Star Alliance, One World, and Sky Team.

Once you are a member, you can book flights with other member airlines and still accumulate points on your airline's mileage program. Sometimes, I even pay a little extra to book a flight with my airline or a member airline to continue to accumulate miles.

Choose a program where your miles *won't* expire.

When I first began to travel for work in 1997, I had enrolled in Lufthansa's Miles and More program. Over the next few years, I realized that the miles I had accumulated came with an expiration date.

Which meant that I could never accumulate enough miles to get a free flight unless I flew far more often.

I changed my membership to the United Mileage Plus program, where my miles never expire. Since then, I have booked *free* international and domestic flights worth thousands of dollars over the years using my miles.

Sign up for the credit card offered by your mileage program

Most major airlines partner with a bank for an airline credit card. Quite often, they offer deals for signing up. I found this deal recently on the American Airlines website:

Earn 50,000 American Airlines

AAdvantage® bonus miles

after **$2,500** in purchases
within the first **3 months** of account opening

Annual fee $99, waived for the first 12 months

Sign up at least *four* months before you leave for your trip and use this card for all your pre-trip shopping. With every dollar you spend, you will gain miles and receive your bonus miles (50,000 in this example). That will be more than enough to get you your first flight out *for free* and still have miles left over.

You can always cancel the card after the first year if you don't want to pay the annual fee. Or ask if it can be waived after the first year. For the past fifteen years, I have been pleased with my United Chase Visa card. I don't mind paying the annual fee because of the benefits I receive.

Layover Lowdown

I love long layovers on international flights. I get to stretch my legs, take a shower, eat proper food, and sleep. When you see a flight with a long layover, e.g., eight hours+, call the airline and ask if they include any free perks such as city tours, hotel stay, food vouchers, etc. Some airlines, such as Singapore Airlines, do.

I once came across a Lufthansa flight with an eighteen-hour layover in Munich and another one with a two-hour layover. Even though Lufthansa did not provide any perks, I picked the one with the overnight layover. I was able to get to Munich downtown with the train from the airport, meet a friend for dinner, and have a relaxed night's sleep. The next morning, I walked to Marienplatz for a lovely morning cappuccino before heading back to the airport in time to catch my next flight segment.

COVID-19 Times Warning:
It may not be the best option during COVID-19 times.

Word of Caution:
If you do take a long layover, make sure your passport will let you leave the airport.

Ensure that your baggage is checked-in all the way to your final destination. What you want is to be able to leave the airport with only your carry-on.

Buying One-way Tickets

I never book round trip flights on my long slow travels because

I never know when I will return and from where. I like being able to take the journey at my own pace without having a return ticket that binds me to a fixed date of return. Before buying a one-way ticket, it is necessary to check: Does the destination country require that you show a return ticket to give you a visa on arrival?

In 2018, I was traveling from Mumbai to Bali. As usual, I had bought a one-way ticket. However, Garuda airlines refused to let me check-in without showing them proof of leaving Indonesia.

My solution?

I bought a fully refundable first-class ticket for a date one month in the future. The airline check-in personnel accepted that. As soon as I landed in Bali, I canceled the ticket and got a full refund.

5 Tips for Finding a Flight Deal

#1 Flexibility, flexibility, flexibility.

The more flexibility you have with your dates, the higher the chances of landing a great flight deal.

- Try different dates around when you want to fly and keep an eye on the fare change trends. **Google Flights** shows you the fares for a whole month in a grid view. With **Skyscanner**, instead of the departure or the return date, choose "Whole month." These options make it very easy to monitor fare change trends and zoom in on that low fare.

- Booking in the low or shoulder season instead of the high season will be kinder to your budget.

- Flying during holidays, such as Thanksgiving or Christmas, when most people are at home with their families, will get you cheaper flights and empty airports.

- If you have flexibility with your dates and your destination, then check websites like **SecretFlying**. They regularly advertise extraordinarily cheap airfares for specific destinations for specific timeframes. Or choose "Everywhere" as your destination in Skyscanner.

- Set up a low fare alert with websites like **airfarwatchdog**, which do a superb job tracking fare changes. It will send you an email/text when it finds the most economical fare for your dates and destination.

 A Quick Tip:

I subscribe to alerts with websites like SecretFlying and airfarewatchdog about two months before I want to fly. Once I have bought the ticket, I unsubscribe myself to reduce digital clutter in my email inbox.

#2 Stitch your flights together.

Break an international flight into its international and regional/domestic sections and then compare fares. Let's pretend that you want to fly from Chicago to the Perhentian islands in Malaysia.

Flight #1   Chicago to Perhentian islands.

Or

Flight #2a   Chicago to Kuala Lumpur
                  with an international airline.
Flight #2b   Kuala Lumpur to Perhentian islands
                  using a regional airline like Air Asia.
"stitch" flight 2a and 2b together.

Which is cheaper?

With option two, you have the added advantage of breaking the journey in Kuala Lumpur for a couple of days. Get over the jet lag and enjoy the nightlife and street food in the Jalan Alor area!

#3 Consider the nickel and dime airlines.

People often skip over these airlines due to their gnarly reputation of tricking customers into paying more by charging extra at every point of sale they can. They bombard you with add-on options like priority boarding, seat selection, insurance, etc., during the booking process.

Don't discard these airlines just yet. These can be great options for domestic or regional flights. In 2018, I booked a flight from Cusco to Lima with Viva Air Peru. Instead of buying the cheapest fare, I purchased the fare one tier up. For a few dollars more, it included one free check-in bag and free airport check-in.

It still turned out cheaper than if I had gone with the lowest airfare with Viva Air and paid extra for a checked-in bag or purchased a flight from a regular airline. That's how you save with nickel and dime airlines.

The most reliable way of finding the nickel and dime airlines that serve a country/region is to do an internet search for *"Budget airlines for <country/continent>."*

 Word of Caution:

Watch out for airlines like Ryanair that might not land at major airports but land/take-off from airports out of the way. They make for some inconvenient and time-consuming airport transfers. It may not be worth the few dollars saved.

#4 Avoid browser tracking and clear the cookies to get better fares.

Airlines and travel discount websites do dynamic pricing based on your location, browser type, and previous itinerary searches. Cookies remember what you searched for in the past. If you repeat the same or similar search over and over again, the website "learns" from your behavior and begins to increase the prices.

To avoid this:

- Delete your internet search history and cookies regularly.
- Use a browser that does not allow tracking, such as Brave. Or set your browser in "incognito" or "private browsing" mode before searching for flights.

How do I do this?

Each browser has a different way of doing this. Doing an internet search for *"deleting tracking history and cookies for <your browser name>"* and *"how to use <your browser name> in incognito mode>"* will get you the right answer for your browser.

#5 Vary the departing and landing airport.

Once, I found the best deal to Kona, Hawaii, not from San Francisco airport, but Oakland airport. The cost and time for getting to either airport by train/bus or Uber was about the same. But the fare difference was a couple of hundred dollars. Needless to say, I booked the flight from Oakland.

And Finally

Once you find a flight that makes you go, "What a steal!":

 Don't wait, book it, and move on.

The Conscious Slow Traveler

#1 Airline carbon offset programs.

Some airlines provide an option to pay a few dollars more towards a carbon offset program, most often, a tree-planting program to encourage "green" and guilt-free flying. However, I will write a few words of caution here. Not all of these programs are credible. During my time in South Africa, I have seen Eucalyptus trees, which are fast-growing, being planted in non-native environments. That harms the local ecology more than benefits it. A quick-fix is not the solution.

Before you pay the extra dollars for these programs:

- Research the credibility of the beneficiary organization.
- When not sure, adopt the policy "Do no harm." Don't opt for the carbon offset program.
- Find other credible ways to offset your flying footprint.

I recommend using emerging websites like **The Good Traveler** to offset your carbon footprint. The Good Traveler uses your dollars in various projects, including waste renewal and green energy and provides complete transparency into the projects they are funding.

Search on the internet for *"How can I offset my flying footprint"* to find alternatives for guilt-free flying.

#2 Make a green choice.

Airlines like KLM, Virgin Air, Qantas Airways, and FinnAir are leading the way to improve their green footprint with a long-term vision of flying carbon-free. Fly with such airlines when possible and let your dollars indirectly contribute towards a greener planet. When signing up for a frequent flyer mileage program, choose an airline that is committed to becoming greener.

Resources

	App	Website	Cost
Online travel discount websites	KAYAK Skyscanner	kayak.com skyscanner.com flights.google.com	Free
Major airline alliances	Star Alliance Navigator	staralliance.com oneworld.com skyteam.com	Free
Low fare alerts		airfarewatchdog.com	Free
Time-bound deals	Secret Flying	secretflying.com	Free
Carbon offset program		thegoodtraveler.org	Free

CHAPTER 10

ACCOMMODATION

December 2009 - Milan, Italy

After living in Milan for a couple of months and exploring the different areas, I had taken a liking to certain neighborhoods in the picturesque city. More than any other, I was utterly drawn to the La Brera area. Its mix of quaint, old, narrow cobblestone streets, ancient architecture combined with boutique shops, and diversity in restaurants and cafes captivated my senses. I was charmed by the way it intertwined old Europe with the modern one. It also hosted the well-known Brera Fine Arts Academy, where I wanted to attend evening classes.

On a Sunday afternoon, after my usual lunch at Rangoli on Via Solferino, I hit the pavement in La Brera. I wanted to soak in the atmosphere by wandering through its streets at a leisurely pace. At the same time, I thought, perhaps, I could begin scouting rental apartments in the area. And so, it happened. There it was. A sign hung on the third floor of an apartment building facade in a classic Milanese style on Via Della Moscova.

> *Apartamento disponibile.*
> *Chiama 1234567*

Bingo!

I immediately dug into my handbag full of random tit-bits and pulled out my phone to take a photo of the sign as a way to record the phone number. Just as I was taking the picture, an old man walked out from under the archway of the building entrance. He looked like he was in his 70's with thick white hair and a twinkle in his brown eyes, almost hidden under massive bushy eyebrows.

"Signora," he said, seeing me taking the photo. "No lo sei-"

"Mi dispiace... Um... Ma non parlo bene l'italiano. Parla inglese?" I quickly blurted out the few Italian phrases I had learned, asking him if he spoke English.

"Ah. Apartamento? Si?" He pointed to the sign.

"Si si," I nodded my head.

"Raffaele," he introduced himself, with a gallant bow.

We began a comical conversation using a combination of broken English and hand gestures. I understood that he was the apartment owner and that the rent was 550 euros per month. My jaw dropped open.

That's cheap for La Brera! Wow! The real estate agents are milking the foreigners here!

Not for a second did I think: *This sounds suspicious.*

"Bene, bene." I managed to get across the message that I wanted to see the apartment.

We climbed the stairs to the third-floor studio apartment from the back of the building. The studio was small with an air of old-Italian charm to it. The walls were painted in red, green, and white—the colors of the Italian flag—and covered with paintings. An ornate king-size bed, two couches, and a dining table with four chairs crowded the tiny studio.

The apartment smelled of freshly brewed coffee.

"Does someone live here?" I asked.

"Yes." Raffaele explained, pointing to his chest, "Io vivo qui."

"So... will you be moving out if I rent the apartment?" I asked, a little perturbed. Was he renting out the place because he needed the money? Or perhaps he was planning to move to the countryside?

"No, no. We share the apartment," he gestured and explained in Italian.

I stared at him in disbelief, thinking I had misunderstood. So, I asked him again.

"I am a very easy-going man, you see. We can also share the bed," he winked.

I stood there in shock. Raffaele intended to rent the apartment to me and share it. I couldn't believe it! How could he even think that to be in the realms of possibility?

I surveyed the fishy sight before me.

No way!

With an abrupt, "No, grazie," I made a swift U-turn and ran down the stairs to Via Della Moscova.

"Signora, signora-"

I heard Raffaele's anxious calls fading as I walked briskly towards the metro station.

> *No more random*
> *apartment hunting*
> *in La Brera.*

I wrote in bold black letters on a post-it and stuck it to the wall above my desk as soon as I returned to the sanctuary of my current apartment on Via Marghera.

* * *

The accommodation you choose is likely to have the most significant effect on the experience of your trip. Most slow travelers will attest to the wisdom of not booking long-term accommodation before seeing the place, exploring the neighborhood, and meeting the landlord. Unless you are confident about your research, have a recommendation from a trusted source, or are not picky at all, don't do it. However, book a roof over your head for the first few days to a few weeks to get you landed in the new place.

Begin with Short-term Accommodation

When it comes to short term accommodation, I've had the best experiences with **Booking** and **Airbnb.** They provide a range of options for all budgets. For a hostel, I begin my search at **Hosteling International, HostelWorld,** and **hostelbookers.** Hostels are a great way to get your foot in the door in a new place. There is no shortage of information available, and it is effortless to meet other travelers, some of who might also be looking for a long-term stay. Join hands and share information.

If you are in the mood to indulge and splurge for your first few days in a new land, then **VRBO** and **VacationHomeRentals** are ideal. These fall in the vacation rental category, where you will pay above the market rate. But the quality of accommodations on offer is also on the high end.

 When booking short-term accommodation, stay closer to the center. You will have easier access to services, information, and avenues to meet people. It helps to get the foot in the door.

Move to Long-term Accommodation

Traveling makes sense only when you have a place to return to. While choosing a long-term accommodation, remember that it will be your base in the new country. Like the spokes in a wheel connected to a center, it will be a sanctuary to return to after short trips and adventures.

Before you book a long-term accommodation, identify your lifestyle needs that will make your stay comfortable and enjoyable. Mine has changed over the years. When I was younger, I was willing to find a room in a shared house or a dorm bed in a hostel. Now I prefer to have my own place.

These are my current requirements.

Must have:

- A private apartment/house furnished with the basics such as a bed, desk, and a couch.

- Private bathroom with hot water unless, I am in a warm, humid area.
- A kitchen equipped with a stove, refrigerator, utensils, cutlery, pots, and pans.
- A good Wi-Fi connection.
- Proper airflow and good natural light.
- A safe neighborhood with easy access to public transportation.
- A little away from crowded, downtown areas and noisy tourist hotspots.
- Access to nature, even if it's a city park or a pathway along a canal.
- Easy access to markets, cafes, restaurants, and other places with social activities.

Nice to have:

- A fireplace, heater, or a fan depending on the weather.
- Weekly cleaning service.

Bonus:

- A garden will clinch the deal.

 What are your requirements?

Convert short-term into long-term stays

If you are happy with your short-term place, then chat with the owner to see if they will consider renting long-term to you. You can negotiate the rent outside the booking platforms, which will save you some rent and the host the cost of the booking platform fees. The longer you stay, the lower the rent will be.

 Word of Caution:
Landlords may not take kindly if you start negotiating a long-term stay with them even before you have begun your short-term stay—or even before booking one.

Homestays

Homestays are the way to go if you want to immerse yourself in the local culture. These will plug you in with the locals right from the start. Another long-term rental might just appear through word-of-mouth and their social network, not to mention the social connections you are likely to make.

Use the website **Homestay** to locate a homestay in the city/country of your interest or ask in the local expat Facebook group.

Word-of-mouth

I had met Elise, a photographer and a web designer, in Peru, in 2018. In one of our online chats, I mentioned that I was planning to go to Guanajuato in November of 2019. She immediately pulled out her Rolodex of travel contacts and sent me her friend Mia's contact information. Mia was from New York, who had made Guanajuato her home for the last six years. A couple of days after I arrived in Guanajuato, I met Mia for a coffee. It turned out that her Mexican landlady, Rosa, had a furnished, light-filled apartment with a stunning view of the city available.

We are all connected by six degrees of separation. Don't be too shy to send a message to your network that you are looking for a long-term rental where you are going. You never know where you might strike gold like I did.

Local expat groups on Facebook & rental agencies

Spread the word in the local expat Facebook group with your housing requirements and budget. Ask for information on the different neighborhoods. You are bound to get a few offers from locals or other foreigners.

Local rental agencies will charge a commission but give you peace of mind and save you a lot of apartment hunting hassle.

Local housing websites

In some countries, there are specific websites the locals use to look for apartments. Such as, in Germany, **wg-gesucht** is popular, while folks in Denmark use **boligportal**. The best way to find these is by asking in the local expat Facebook group or your local short-term landlord. They will be able to point you to the most commonly used websites.

These will be in the local language and may or may not have an English version. Enlist a local's or other traveler's help for translating these or pull out that Google translator app. It's time to start sinking your teeth into the local lingo!

Become a long-term hotel guest

If you are traveling in the off-season when the hotels are likely to have unoccupied rooms, locate a hotel you like and negotiate with the manager for an extended stay (three months or longer). Watch the price drop with breakfast and weekly cleaning service included! You might even luck out in a luxury suite.

Hit the pavement

Go for a stroll in the neighborhoods you like and look for "Accommodation Available" signs posted in cafes, yoga studios, marketplaces, university areas, etc. This strategy will not work in all countries. In Denmark, this is not a common way to look for accommodation, but in Peru or Mexico, this method works. I wasn't lucky in my attempt in Milan. But some other slow travelers I have met have found their perfect spot this way.

Craigslist & Facebook Marketplace

Craigslist is a nonprofit website to find accommodation and many other services for several countries. I've had excellent luck finding apartments through Craigslist in the USA. Since these listings are by the owners or lease management companies, the rents tend to be reasonable and local. **Facebook Marketplace** is similar to Craigslist, but is on Facebook.

5 Ways to Find Free Accommodation

#1 Couch surfing

Locals and expats interested in meeting and hosting travelers for short-term post advertisements on **CouchSurfing**. These accommodations are free but are usually meant for the short term. If you are nimble and don't mind being mobile, you can couch surf your way through your entire slow travel for free and make many new friends along the way.

A long-term rental might just fall into your lap through the people you meet while couch surfing!

#2 Pet sitting/House sitting

Pet sitting/House sitting is another way to find free accommodation. These jobs could be for anywhere between a few days to a few months. You can find some very nice house sitting/pet sitting opportunities if you are flexible with your dates.

Search for *"pet sitting <country/city>"* or *"house sitting <country/ city>"* on Facebook. **Nomador** and **HouseSitter** are other useful websites for finding house sitting/pet sitting opportunities.

#3 Volunteering or Voluntourism

Volunteering for an NGO or commercial enterprise is another way to find free accommodation. More on this in Chapter 11: Earn While You Travel.

#4 Exchange your home for another

Let's say you have a home in Santorini, Greece, and want to live in New York City for a few months. **HomeExchange** is a website where you can find someone who wants to do the opposite of what you want to do—someone has a home in New York City and wants to live in Santorini for a few months.

If you are a homeowner, this idea may sound a bit risky. Even though HomeExchange is a reliable, legitimate website, that doesn't mean you should not take precautions and thoroughly investigate a potential exchanger. Chat with the exchanger over Skype or Zoom to get a sense of them and their place. Establish a comfort zone before agreeing to an exchange.

#5 Host a sister group on Facebook

If you are a solo woman traveler and want to connect with other women, post a message in the "Host a Sister" group on Facebook for a short-term stay. It's another way to get started and meet with the locals while looking for long-term accommodation.

4 Tips for Finding a Budget Accommodation

#1 The longer you stay, the lower the rent.

A month-long stay is cheaper than a week-long stay. A stay for a few months is even less expensive. Smart landlords will prefer to keep their place occupied for a few months at a reduced rent instead of having gaps in the rentals. Negotiation is key.

#2 Rent from the locals.

Renting directly from a local owner is a cheaper alternative than going through a real estate agency or a booking platform. Cut the middle man out and rent straight from a local.

But first, meet the landlord and talk face to face. You will be able to verify that the landlord and the place are genuine.

#3 Pay by cash.

In some places, landlords prefer to get the rent in cash instead of with a credit card. In other places, they will *only* accept cash. Paying in cash can reduce your rent. Paying cash upfront for a few months at a time can get you an even deeper discount.

#4 Get an apartment where the locals live.

Most places on the tourist track will have areas where the tourists hang out and other areas where the locals live. The tourist areas are, without saying, expensive. The local areas tend to have more normal rental prices. Of course, it can also happen that your local landlord may charge you higher than local rents simply because you are a foreigner, but it will still be cheaper than in the tourist areas.

These areas tend to be a little outside the tourist hotspots, but you will be living there and not just checking off a bucket list, right? What better way than to plop yourself in a local area and live as the locals do?

An ideal neighborhood is the one which has a mix of locals and foreigners living there.

Before You Book...

Read reviews if available.

You will learn more about what worked and what did not straight from the horse's mouth. Once through an Airbnb room review, I discovered that there were no windows in the room I was about to book. Needless to say, I did not book the room.

Chat with the landlord.

Don't be shy. It is important to establish a rapport with the landlord if you are booking a place for an extended stay. If you sense that the owner is not responsive or forthcoming with information, drop that place like a hot potato.

Scout neighborhoods.

Do some initial research on the different neighborhoods and explore these areas. Is there a particular place you intend to go to daily? Such as a co-working space or a yoga studio or an NGO that you'll be volunteering at? Understanding your daily routine and habits will help to narrow down the areas to search for long-term accommodation.

Smell a Scam

I was introduced to Vidya by Martin. I had met Martin during a brief stay at the Ramana Maharshi ashram in South India in 2010, where he is a long-time resident monk. Vidya was coming to Copenhagen for an internship with the EEA (European Environmental Agency). He asked me if I could help her in her search for accommodation in Copenhagen.

I was more than happy to help out!

I emailed her the various websites that she could use to find a shared apartment in Copenhagen. I also suggested searching on Craigslist but warned her to be careful since it's an unregulated website. That means no one can be held accountable for imposters posting fake listings. A couple of months went by. Since I had not heard from Vidya, I assumed that she did not need more help from me.

On a fine summer afternoon, I was casually hanging out at the street party on Dronning Louises bridge on one of the lakes in Copenhagen. It is not uncommon to see the Danes rejoicing and soaking in the long Nordic summer days after months of the short and dark winter gloom. The Dronning Louises bridge is one such place in Copenhagen where friends gather with boxes of Tuborg or Carlsberg beers and music systems to simply hang out and bask in the light. At times, I have even seen a wedding reception take place on the bridge what with tables, chairs, cutlery, champagne, and roses elegantly laid out while the groom arrives with his bride on a Christiania bicycle!

I received a frantic call from Vidya. She was stranded in Copenhagen, and could I come to pick her up? Feeling a little anxious, I hopped on my bicycle and made my way to the address she had given me. There she was—standing with her bags, all alone, just arrived from India, and looking extremely worried.

In between sobs, she explained that she had booked an apartment through Craigslist. Upon landing in Copenhagen, when she got to the address given to her, there was no apartment there to her utter dismay and shock! Only some shops.

"The rent was so cheap! I thought I had hit the jackpot," she managed to whimper while sobbing.

Oh, no!

"I even paid two months' worth of rent as a deposit and the first month's rent. The owner said that the apartment's caretaker would come to hand me the keys. But there is no one here. I have been waiting for two hours. I can't reach the owner on email or phone, either."

"How did you send him the money?" I took the last chance to see whether we could salvage the situation in any way.

"By Western Union."

That's it. There was no way she was going to get her money back.

Long story short, I managed to settle her in an apartment with another girl, but she never got her lost money back.

These types of scams have been known to have happened. I have heard of other situations where the landlord meets the renter, collects the rent, and hands over the keys. You might think everything is in order, except when ten other people show up who have also been rented the same apartment by the same scam-artist.

 Word of Caution:

Don't book accommodation through unregulated sources like Craigslist and Facebook Marketplace without seeing the place and meeting the landlord.

Here are some simple things to look out for:

- Are photos of the apartment/room/house you want to rent of good quality?
- Check on Google Maps for the exact location. Does your research indicate that it is a good neighborhood?
- Ask questions about the neighborhood, such as the closest markets, cafes, pharmacy, and public transportation.
- If the rent is considerably cheaper than similar other listings in that area, don't get excited. Instead, get suspicious and ask the advertiser directly why the rent is so low.
- If the advertiser has a story about how they are stuck somewhere in another part of the world due to a family emergency or some such personal reason, but a local housekeeper will hand you the keys and the documents, alarm bells should be going off.
- If the advertiser asks you to pay any part of the rent or deposit remotely, via a cash transfer such as Western Union, *don't do it*. Agree to pay the full rent and deposit only upon arrival, seeing the place, and getting the keys. If the advertiser sounds genuine to you, agree to pay a very small deposit to reserve the spot. Good landlords will not press you for the rent but will let you settle in comfortably for a couple of days before asking for the rent.

The Conscious Slow Traveler

#1 Go local.

Reject big tourism, big brands, and international chains whenever possible. Let more of your money go straight into the pockets of the locals by renting accommodation directly from them.

#2 Stay at earth-friendly hotels and accommodations.

Emerging websites such as **B'n'Tree, Fairbnb** (available only in Europe at the time of writing this book), and **GreenKey** are committed to providing earth-friendly accommodation. **Hosteling International** has long held the ethos of being eco-friendly.

Besides these platforms, there is an emerging trend of eco-friendly resorts and accommodation. "Eco" and "Green" have become marketing buzzwords to attract travelers who want to make conscious choices. Beware of fake "eco" and "green" accommodations. Be sure to ask them what makes them "eco" or "green"? Ask for information on their recycling program, whether they use renewable energy sources, waste management, and so on before making a booking.

#3 Reduce your energy consumption.

When staying at a hotel or in a serviced apartment where they provide a daily cleaning service, ask to change the sheets and towels weekly or biweekly.

Air conditioning comes at a considerable cost to the environment. Try to find accommodation without air conditioning if you are in a hot and humid region. Leave the windows open or use fans instead. If the heat is unbearable and you must have air conditioning, then reduce the amount of time you turn it on.

Turn off the lights, fan, and air conditioner when you leave your room and limit your energy use. Whether you pay for it or not, the environment will pay for it.

#4 Give back by leaving a review.

I cannot emphasize enough how vital it is to leave an honest review for the bookings you made through a booking platform. It should include what you did and did not like. Many travelers prefer to write only positive reviews, but your honest review gives the host feedback on how to improve their accommodations and services and keeps them accountable. It also informs other travelers about details that will make it easier for them to pick the right accommodation. Give back to the travel community.

Resources

	App	Website	Cost
Booking websites	Booking.com Airbnb	booking.com airbnb.com bedandtree.com fairbnb.coop greenkey.global	Free or a small service fee.
Hostels	Hostelworld Hostelbookers. com	hostelworld.com hihostels.com hostelbookers.com	Free
Vacation rentals	Vrbo Vacation Rentals	vrbo.com vacationhomerentals. com	Free
Housesitting/ Pet sitting	Nomador Trusted-House-Sitters	nomador.com trustedhousesitters.com	Free
Free accom- modation	HomeExchange	homeexchange.com Host a Sister group on Facebook	Free
	Couchsurfing Travel App	couchsurfing.com	Charges a small subscription to help them during COVID-19 times.
Home stays	Homestay	homestay.com	Free
Unregulated websites		Facebook Marketplace craigslist.org	Free

CHAPTER 11

EARN WHILE YOU TRAVEL

"We have a consulting assignment for you in Dublin, Ireland. Interested?" A short message beeped on my phone at 5:00 a.m. It was Ray, one of my ex-colleagues. I had been pursuing a conversation with him for a few months about potential projects in Europe. As I was keen to live in Europe at that time, the answer to his question was a no-brainer.

5:05 a.m: "Yes. Details, please." I sent a short reply.

5:10 a.m: "Start time in one week. The consulting duration will be four months, with the possibility of an extension. All expenses paid. If yes, check your email for more details," came the reply.

5:11 a.m: "Yes."

The project details arrived in my email inbox at 5:30 a.m. After a brief round of negotiation over email, by 11:00 a.m., we had signed a contract. The next week saw a two-day training in Minneapolis, packing up my home, packing for the trip, organizing the logistics, and flying to Dublin.

Conversations and follow-ups over four months had culminated into a contract within a few hours. What began as a four-month gig in Dublin continued to become one and a half years in Milan on a different deal. One contract led to another. In 2011, I formally relocated to Denmark and established an independent consulting business in Copenhagen. Assignments enabled me to live and work in Milan, Helsinki, Kuala Lumpur, London, and the USA while maintaining a quasi-permanent base in Copenhagen.

I worked while I traveled and I traveled while I worked.

* * *

Slow travel is first about courage and curiosity and then about money. But the reality is that we all have bills to pay. Some slow travelers solve this by doing the work-save-travel-repeat loop. This is how Glen, a handyman from Denver, Colorado sorts this out:

> *"My girlfriend and I work to travel. About every four years, we quit our jobs, rent our house, and travel for six months to a year. We have spent months in SE Asia as well as travels in Latin America."*

I have been able to fulfill my dream of traveling with work because my skills in the technology sector are global and portable. However, that may not be the case for everyone.

If you are thinking, *"If only I could pay my way through my travels,"* then this is the chapter for you.

Without further ado, let's dive in.

Out of Sight is *Not* Out of Mind

Many people get stuck believing that out of sight is out of mind. If you take a longer than expected break, you will be rejected by your industry upon return. I will not challenge that by saying it's *never* true. However, with a certain degree of confidence, I will say that it is not *always* true. I took a two-year unpaid sabbatical from my career from 2002 to 2004, and another two-and-a-half-year sabbatical from 2006 to the end of 2008. Each time, I have rejoined the technology sector with an even better job opportunity than before. At present, I am enjoying a break for five years and counting.

From my own experience, I have found that employers value people with diverse life experiences, and slow travel *is* considered as an enriching one. My new employers were rather impressed that I had taken the chance to take a break and embarked on a journey of discovery.

Confidence is a highly desired quality. Do you believe in yourself and what you have to offer?

I certainly don't suggest that you throw caution to the wind, quit your job, and take off. But don't be stuck in the mindset of "out of sight is out of mind" either. Evaluate the possibility of taking a sabbatical—paid or unpaid—from working life.

Take Your Job Remote

Many companies are recognizing the relationship between working from home and higher productivity. New technologies are making it more and more possible to work remotely. Meetings can be held over online conference call portals like **Zoom** and **Jitsi**. Remote teams and projects can be managed using tools like **Monday**, **Asana**, and **teamwork.**

- Are you in a profession where you can work remotely?
- Can you convince your manager to let you do so?
- Can you work remotely for a while and then return to the office?
- Can you work remotely for three months, make a two-week trip back to the office for any face-to-face requirements, and repeat?

Professions like editor, writer, program manager, designer, coder, online marketing, customer support, teacher, accountant, data entry, social media manager, etc., are well suited for remote work. Others like a nurse, doctor, working in a manufacturing unit, etc., are not.

Many companies who were previously reluctant to let their employees work from home even when possible, are now allowing that to happen in the wake of the COVID-19 pandemic. Twitter has become the first major U.S. tech company to allow its employees to work remotely and indefinitely. Mark Zuckerberg, CEO of Facebook, has declared that they are "aggressively opening up remote hiring." They expect that about half of its workforce will work remotely over the next five to ten years, permanently!

We can certainly expect this trend to gain momentum in the post-COVID-19 world. Why not take advantage of this opportunity and take the leap to live out your dreams of travel while continuing your career?

Get Transferred Overseas

I almost did it back in 2000. At that time, I was working for a multinational company in the Silicon Valley of California. During my first overseas work trip to Jerusalem, I was mesmerized by the city. There was something inexplicable about it that made me want to go back. I broached the topic with my manager upon return. He agreed. I could continue to work for him from the Jerusalem office for two years. In the end, life happened, and I couldn't take up the opportunity.

Perhaps you can get yourself transferred to one of your company's overseas offices for some time?

Dive into the Location Independent Free-lance/Gig Economy

Use your skills to do freelance work and take gigs (full-time or part-time) while on the road.

A brief recently published by **CIO Dive**, a website that provides insights and trends shaping the IT industry expects the gig economy, where small packages of work are outsourced to remote freelancers, to grow in the post-COVID-19 world. Can you work freelance and be location independent? If you are a graphic designer, book cover creator, blogger, virtual assistant, market research specialist, journalist, photographer, author, coder, etc., *you can*.

Upwork and **Fiverr** are popular sites for marketing your freelance services. Other websites to look for remote work are **Toptal, peopleperhour, weworkremotely,** and **guru**. Facebook groups such as Remote Jobseeker, Digital Nomads, Remote Job Opportunities are also useful resources to look for remote gigs, connect with other remote job seekers, and watch trends.

Become an Entrepreneur, Start Your Own Business

I met Anja in the Sacred Valley of the Incas, Peru, in 2017. At that time, she was undergoing a training program to become a life coach. She was changing her career direction.

"I can't afford to live in the Netherlands while I am studying for my life coaching certification and building up a coaching practice. Most of the courses are online. About every three months, I have to attend a one-week session in person. So, I prefer to live here. Moreover, I love my life here in the Sacred Valley!"

Amit is an entrepreneur and a surfing buff working on his first start-up company from Puerto Escondido, Mexico.

"I am trying to start my company in California, and my team is in Asia. I am on a cash crunch, and it's cheaper to live here. Plus, I love to surf—that's what I do on the weekends. Find the different surfing spots around here. Life can't get any better than this for me right now."

Like Antja and Amit, you can also become an entrepreneur. Start that business you always wanted to while slow traveling.

Give Back by Volunteering or Voluntourism

According to the NGO Save the Children, the world's leading independent organization for children, "voluntourism" is one of the fastest-growing travel trends with 1.6 million people volunteering overseas each year. The trend is increasing every year.

As a volunteer, you will most likely not earn any income but will almost always get free accommodation. That is a saving of 30% to 40% of your monthly budget right there. Apart from that, volunteering projects provide an enriching and eye-opening experience into the local culture.

Before signing up for a project, look for:

- Projects that are beneficial to the community. Is the help being rendered in collaboration with local people instead of being imposed on them?
- Projects that have long-term goals and which empower the local community to take charge after you leave for continual benefit.

- Projects that provide you with a learning experience while helping.

- Details about accommodation and food arrangements. Don't expect luxury in volunteer projects, but ensure that your basic needs will be met well enough to be productive.

- Projects that don't ask you to pay for volunteering. Sounds odd? It did to me when I first heard about a retreat center in the Peruvian Amazon asking volunteers to pay in return for volunteering. Don't reject this option immediately though. Evaluate whether the skills you will gain justify the cost? Then make a decision.

If you are already in town, meet the people offering the volun-tourism in person to see if the chemistry is right. Nothing beats a real face-to-face conversation.

WorkAway is a well-known website for travelers looking to cut their traveling costs while beneficially engaging their time. Note that WorkAway projects are not limited to only NGOs or not-for-profit organizations. It also includes projects by for-profit enterprises such as hostels, guesthouses, eco-agriculture projects, and private people looking for help in their house or language and cultural exchange.

Are you interested in learning about and immersing yourself in sustainability practices? The **Global Eco-village Network** provides a comprehensive listing of eco-villages worldwide with detailed information and how you can volunteer.

Other popular sites to look for volunteer opportunities are **Idealist, HelpX, HelpStay,** and **WWOOF**. Connect with expats and other travelers through the local expat group on Facebook and spread the word that you are looking to volunteer.

The volunteer opportunity could end up becoming a new career if you find an NGO that stirs up your passions!

Teach English as a Foreign Language

Teaching English online to children in East Asia or business English to adults in Japan, Latin America, France, Germany, etc., has been on the rise in the last few years. It has gained popularity with many slow travelers and rightly so. This is why:

- You are your own boss. You can choose the hours and days you want to teach. You get paid for the number of hours you teach. Do you want to earn more? Then teach more. Do you want to spend more time diving? Then teach less.

- It's straightforward to get into this line of work. You can get started in less than a month, and within one to three months, you can reach an income that is sufficient to support yourself.

- You can work from anywhere you want!

You need only three things to begin teaching online:

#1 A laptop

#2 A reliable high-speed internet connection

#3 An English language teaching certification

VIPKids, Teachaway, DaDa, GoGoKid, and **iTutorGroup** are popular websites for teaching children. **Learnship** and **Fluentify** are recommended for business English for companies. Once you have gathered some teaching experience through these or other companies, you can market yourself on portals like **takelessons, Verbling,** and **Italki** for freelance English teaching gigs. **Good Air Language** provides an excellent consolidated list of companies to apply for online English teaching jobs.

Start digging, and you will find many more.

In-person English teaching opportunities

Dave's ESL Café, "the Internet's Meeting Place for ESL + EFL teachers + students from around the world," has been a long-standing institution by itself in the world of teaching English as a foreign language. It has been a go-to whether you are looking to hire an English language teacher or you are a teacher looking for a job in a foreign country.

English language certifications

Whether you teach English online or in-person, you will need a certification to establish your credibility. **TEFL** (Teaching English as a Foreign Language), **TOEFL** (Test of English as a Foreign Language), **IELTS** (International English Language Testing System), and **CELTA** (Certificate in Teaching English to Speakers of Other Languages) are well-known and well-accepted credentials.

Before getting a certification, check with the work opportunities you are interested in about which one is acceptable to them.

Turn What You Know into an Opportunity to Teach

Ask yourself, what skills do you have that you can share with others while on the road? Are you a yoga teacher? A Tai-chi expert? A surfer? A dance and movement teacher? An artist? A chef? A gardener? Could you teach or offer these skills while on the slow travel trail? I have seen many travelers offer classes and workshops.

Some have created online training programs using online teaching portals like **Udemy, Lynda,** and **MasterClass**. Their advertising motto is: "Learn anytime, anywhere at your own pace." You can offer your courses through these portals at very reasonable prices and earn an income for every person who signs up.

Become a Digital Nomad

Digital nomadism is a trend that has been on the rise in recent years. A whole new subculture within the slow travel movement has evolved. What sets this subculture apart from the rest, is as the name implies—digital nomads. **Investopedia,** one of the best-known sources of financial information on the internet, defines a Digital Nomad as:

> *An individual who works remotely using information and communications technology may work out of cafes, on beaches or in hotel rooms as they are not tied to a location. They tend to be tech-forward and ambitious, working mainly in IT, creative or knowledge economy.*

All they need is a fast Wi-Fi connection, a laptop, and a smartphone to work. Digital nomads are usually found doing tech/digital jobs such as SEO marketing, Amazon FBA selling, programming, cryptocurrency trading, web designing, online marketing to name a few, while traveling at their own pace.

Connect to the community of worldwide digital nomads through Facebook groups like Digital Nomads Hub, Digital Nomad Entrepreneurs, and many more. Merely doing a Facebook search for *"digital nomads"* will give you a few groups to join.

Co-working Spaces

A co-working space is a well-equipped office space shared with others. Instead of signing an office lease for yourself, you sign up for a daily, weekly, or monthly subscription to use the shared office space. It works out cheaper since you are not saddled with the costs of setting up an office space such as signing a lease, purchasing a desk, chair, internet connection, etc. It's also easier to move on to your next destination without having to deal with rental leases and selling furniture.

Using a co-working space keeps one foot loose and free while having a semiformal working space in an environment that keeps you focused. It provides all the amenities needed to conduct your business such as fast and reliable Wi-Fi, private or shared desks, meeting rooms for conference calls, silent zones, cafeteria, and at times a kitchen.

What I found the most enriching during the time I had signed up at **Hubud** in Ubud and **Dojo** in Canggu (both in Bali) were the *free* workshops on different topics that a member with experience provided for others. I learned a lot about cryptocurrencies, Amazon FBA selling, drop shipping, and digital marketing by attending these workshops.

Plus, you will meet some fascinating people with innovative ways of earning a living.

 Did I mention that it beats the loneliness that comes from working remotely?

Simply Being!

If you are coming out of a hectic and stressful on-the-go career or an emotionally intense time, then all you may want is to simply inhale and exhale, one breath at a time, without any schedules or to-do lists.

By the time 2015 came around, I was up to my ears with flights, airports, hotels, and flying to new cities for consulting projects with different clients and deadlines. My slow travel-for-work life had changed into a fast travel-for-work life. After I wrapped up my consulting business at the end of 2015, the last thing I wanted was a schedule and getting onto an airplane. My body, mind, and soul craved still moments in the garden with a coffee for a few hours and soaking in the early morning sunshine. That is all I did in the house I rented in Pisac, Peru, for four months.

I didn't earn any money. But I won my soul back. Slowing down, dropping into the **Now**, and reconnecting with myself was my income. I rediscovered myself on silent walks in the mountains and watching the ordinariness of everyday life unfold from an upstairs cafe overlooking the Plaza de Armas while sipping multiple cups of *Koka** tea. And I began to paint again.

 Don't let anyone guilt you into believing you ought to be busy doing something all the time.

Give yourself the gift of simply being. Sometimes, that is what our soul needs.

Making Sense of Visas Again & Taxes

At this point, you might be wondering what type of visa slow travelers use while working on the road?

The answer is: a tourist/visitor visa.

Most slow travelers who work while they travel are on a tourist/visitor visa with their business/freelance work based in their home country, which is also where they pay taxes. That is fine so

---

*   *Koka,* leaves native to Western South America used to alleviate altitude sickness and an important part of the Andean cosmology and ceremonies

long as you are not setting up a business or getting employed in a foreign country.

Let's say you decide to open a café, a shop, or establish another type of business in the foreign country. That is not possible on a tourist/visitor visa. You will need to explore the different types of visas and how to qualify for those. Every country has its own work/business visa requirements. The most reliable source of information is the country's consulate.

If you are getting yourself transferred to one of your company's overseas offices, your company should take care of any visa requirements.

Resources

	App	Website	Cost
Freelance work	Upwork Fiverr Toptal Talent PeoplePerHour	upwork.com fiverr.com guru.com toptal.com peopleperhour.com weworkremotely.com	The freelancer is charged a commission.
Online English teaching	VIPKid Teach DaDa Teacher GOGOKid Teach Fluentify Business TakeLessons for Teachers italki Verbling	vipkid.com teachaway.com dadaabc.com/en.html itutorgroup.com teacher.gogokid.com learnship.com fluentify.com takelessons.com italki.com verbling.com goodairlanguage.com	Free
English language certifications		ielts.org ets.org/toefl tefl.com cambridgeenglish. org/teaching-english/ teaching-qualifica- tions/celta/	Fee for appearing for the exam.
In-Person English language teaching		eslcafe.com	Free
Create your online teaching programs	Lynda.com Udemy Online Video Course Udemy for Business MasterClass: Learn New Skills	lynda.com udemy.com masterclass.com	Fees for using their online portal.
Volunteer	Workaway Travel App	workaway.info helpx.net helpstay.com wwoof.net ecovillage.org idealist.org	Different models.

SECTION III

A ROMANCE BEGINS

We travel, initially, to lose ourselves; and we travel, next to find ourselves. We travel to open our hearts and eyes and learn more about the world than our newspapers will accommodate. We travel to bring what little we can, in our ignorance and knowledge, to those parts of the globe whose riches are differently dispersed. And we travel, in essence, to become young fools again - to slow time down and get taken in, and fall in love once more.

Pico Iyer

CHAPTER 12

IS IT SAFE?

A country I never wanted to go to but had to.

Spending a five-month-long semester at the University of Kwa-Zulu Natal in Durban as part of the program I was enrolled in at the University of Freiburg in Germany, was mandatory.

"You do know that South Africa has a high number of violent crimes?" some friends expressed their concern.

Yes, I had read the crime statistics. Out of fear, I almost wrote a letter to the Program Director at the university.

"Dear Prof. Meyer,

Due to an emergency of extreme distress and under duress, I am requesting permission to be exempted from going to South Africa and instead complete the program requirements here in Freiburg."

I knew what he would say, so I didn't.

I settled in a luxury house shared by eleven other students. It came with a security wall, a code to get in, a swimming pool, and two African maids who made an hour-long journey each way from their settlements to clean and cook in the house. Over time, I learned that apartheid had been abolished—but only legally.

Upon arrival, the university handed us a welcome packet. Amongst other information, it included two condoms and a pamphlet explaining the importance of condoms in preventing HIV. That didn't help alleviate my anxiety.

Over the next few days, my housemates instructed me on "The don'ts of life in Durban."

"Don't walk alone before 9 a.m. or after 6 p.m."

"Do *not* take the shared taxis. Always call a private taxi recommended by someone you know."

"Don't *ever* travel by train."

"Keep a pepper spray with you at all times."

"Don't hang around the same place for too long. You'll get noticed and targeted."

"*Never* go anywhere alone. Always keep company."

The next few months felt like forced confinement.

"I can't live here!" I cried while unpacking reluctantly.

At the same time, I mused, "So many people live here and go about their days and lives despite the crime. *If they can do it, so can I.*"

To start with, I devised my own safety ground rules for using a shared taxi.

- Don't get into a shared taxi if it has only one or two people in it or if it's empty.
- Sit as close to the door as possible.
- Only use them during the day. Avoid taxis during public holidays or evening times.
- Only use them within Durban's inner city and not for going to the suburbs. Call a private taxi for longer trips.
- Avoid shared taxis with only men in them. Don't make eye contact with the people in the cab, especially the men.

Trust me when I say that I was not being paranoid. Over time, my confidence increased each time I took a shared taxi without an incident.

A couple of months later, I became more adventurous and did the unthinkable. Two shared taxis and four hours later, I reached the Drakensberg Mountains on the edge of the Kingdom of Lesotho. I even found the courage to take a night bus from Johannesburg to Durban using a bus line favored by the locals. The final icing on the cake was taking a bus from Durban to Umtata and waiting at the Umtata gas station alone for five hours before the Bulungula ecolodge staff arrived to pick me up! One could reach the Bulungula ecolodge on the Wild Coast of Eastern Cape only by a few hours of off-roading in an SUV.

I can't pinpoint exactly when it happened.

Perhaps it was while tracking a leopard in Kruger National Park at dusk. Or maybe it was while I was sitting in a crowded shanty room with the local healer and herbalist that our maids took me to, watching her perform healing rituals. I am sure that something stirred within me as I walked in the township of Soweto. The girly camaraderie shared with the *Xhosa** girls in *Nqileni*† village when they gave me a makeover by putting a local mud mask on my face and braiding my hair in a cornrow style while I was trying my best to sip down the nasty tasting, frothy *umqombothi*‡ showed me that we are not so different after all.

Alluring, complicated, dynamic, heart-wrenching, and magnificent, South Africa had cast its magic spell over me. What had been a prejudiced start—I shamefully admit—laden with fear and reluctance had metamorphosed into a passionate love affair. The realization came unannounced and hit me like a tsunami.

"I don't want to leave." I concluded while packing reluctantly. For the first time, I felt the heartache of loving a place and leaving it—a country I did not want to leave but had to.

* * *

Is falling in love safe? It's not. It comes packaged with the fear of heartbreak.

Does that stop you from falling in love all over again? I hope your answer is NO!

If slow travel is like a love affair, then I hope fears will not stop you from taking a leap of faith into this whirlwind romance.

---

* *Xhosa*, a Bantu ethnic group whose homeland is in the modern-day Eastern Cape region of South Africa
† *Nqileni*, a small village tucked away on the far eastern cape of South Africa
‡ *umqombothi*, a local beer made from maize and sorghum

Overcoming Fear

It is only apt to quote Nelson Mandela at this point:

> *I learned that courage was not the absence of fear, but the triumph over it. The brave man is not he who does not feel afraid, but he who conquers that fear.*

You see, fear can either paralyze us or act as a catalyst that pushes us to find our way. What spurs me on is the fact that so many people face danger every day but their lives do not come to a standstill. If they can keep going, so can I. That doesn't mean that I would intentionally go to a country like Afghanistan or Syria during wartime to prove a point. It means that I make informed decisions.

You see, the notion of security is a relative concept. The amount of fear associated with safety depends on where you are from. If you grew up under the threat of getting bombed every day of your life, India would be a piece of cake for you. But if you grew up in Western Europe, India might feel dangerous to some.

More often than not, the reality on the ground is not as bad as how it is portrayed by the media. Contrary to what many people think, the rest of the world is not full of dangerous people trying to rob you, kill you, molest you, etc.

I resonate with how the Swedish cyclist, Emma, dealt with the notions of fear and safety.

> *"Cycling, as a solo female through South America, did make many people question my sanity. Many people connect this continent with kidnapping, rapes, murders, and drug trafficking because of the media. They were, therefore, convinced that this was not such a great idea. I did not want to let fear for any of these reasons stop me from fulfilling my dream. Instead, I searched for confirmation of what I so genuinely wanted to believe. Most people you meet don't want to kill you. They are just pleased to be able to help you. After having spent eighteen months on this continent, I did manage to confirm this for myself and worried family members on numerous occasions."*

From my time in South Africa, I learned that it is essential to keep an open mind even about countries that you might be worried about as long as they aren't officially designated unsafe by your home government. That said, there are some things you need to be aware of and can do to stay safe when traveling in foreign countries.

13 Simple Points for Safe Travels

First things first:

Add the police/emergency number to your phone or set it to speed dial.

Let at least one person in your life know where you are and where you will be going.

#1 Keep track of travel advisories, news, and alerts.

Natural disasters, disease epidemics, or political instability can strike unexpectedly. For official travel advisories, check the travel warnings issued by your home country. I find the **British Foreign Travel Advice** to be concise and realistic. Post questions on the local expat group on Facebook to learn about the on-the-ground news and safety issues from people living there.

Ultimately, trust your instincts. We tend to dismiss that little voice inside us as silly.

Oh! Don't be paranoid!

But that little voice is what keeps us safe. If your instincts say don't go then—Don't go.

#2 Investigate the don'ts about the place.

Is it safe to walk alone on the streets after 7 p.m? Is it safe to take taxis at night? What areas/neighborhoods should you avoid? Again, I find the local expat group on Facebook to be the best source of information for this.

#3 Take taxis that are recommended.

When taking local taxis, take recommended taxi companies, even if they are a little more expensive. Ask your landlord or post a question in the local expat group on Facebook for recommendations.

#4 Follow local dress code customs.

While following the appropriate dress code is advised to avoid cultural faux pas, it is also recommended for safety. Clothes that reveal skin are entirely acceptable and normal in western countries. But they could pose a danger in countries like India or the Middle East. This point is a particularly important point for women traveling solo.

#5 Take a working phone when going to remote areas.

If you are using your phone service from back home, remember to turn your roaming service ON and take your charger with you.

#6 Become familiar with the local currency.

Sometimes, cashiers hope that if you're paying a tiny amount with a large note, you might not notice a discrepancy of a few coins in the change they return to you. It can be confusing when paying two million for a bag of potatoes with a fifty million note. We can get lost in the zeroes and the coins—petty theft at its best, but it does happen. It's not a big amount of money, but we encourage this behavior by not calling it out.

#7 Don't carry a load of cash with you when you're going about your day.

When going to the supermarket, laundry service, restaurant, hike, etc., only take enough cash as you think you might need plus a tad bit more. Keep the rest of the cash safe in your house.

#8 Be on alert in crowded places.

Crowded bus stations, buses, train stations, trains, marketplaces, and streets are playgrounds for thieves and pickpockets. Use a money belt under your shirt/top when out and about in busy places. When walking with a daypack, wear it in the front instead of on the back. I learned this the hard way when in 2009 my wallet got stolen from my daypack in a jam-packed metro during rush hour in downtown Milan. I was left with only a few coins in my pocket.

When paying cash, don't pull out a wad of money at once. Split the money you are carrying in different pockets and pull money out only from one place at a time.

#9 Stay 'tethered' to your belongings while on a journey in trains/buses.

Don't leave them unguarded and go for a stroll. If you are changing buses/trains and there is a luggage transfer involved, keep your eyes on your bags if possible.

#10 Don't invite temptation.

When you leave your house, don't leave your valuables like electronics, cash, jewelry, etc., in such a way that a passerby can spot them easily through a window and get tempted to break in.

#11 Make a copy of essential documents and information.

This includes your passport, driver's license, insurance cards, credit cards, and phone numbers to call in case of theft—and keep them somewhere safe. If your apartment does not have a safe, you can take a more creative approach. I keep them between layers of my clothes or under the mattress.

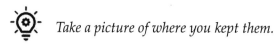 *Take a picture of where you kept them.*

After a few months, it is easy to forget that you have copies of vital documents under the mattress when you are packing to leave!

#12 Solo women traveling can get hassled by men.

In cultures that are considered patriarchal, it is uncustomary for a woman to travel solo. In these cultures, men are not used to proximity with women outside of their families. They can take it as a signal that you are "available." You can be subjected to eve-teasing, catcalling, or get propositioned outright.

While it seldom leads to a dangerous situation, it's best to steer clear of it by following local dress codes and behavior customs. If you find yourself in such circumstances, simply walk on and don't engage. At times, I have lied and said that I'm engaged or married. In Turkey, I even wore a fake ring on my wedding finger to deter men!

#13 KNOW the rules and FOLLOW them.

If you're traveling to countries that restrict personal freedom like North Korea and China or to countries known to be in a state of conflict (Israel, Palestine, or Syria), learn the rules and follow them.

- Don't criticize the local regime in public, to a local, or on social media.

- Don't take photos of people without their permission. Even better, don't take pictures of people at all, especially if you plan to post them on social media. You will leave when your trip is over, but the person whose photo you took and posted on social media could get into trouble.

 Keep your wits about you and travel safe!

CHAPTER 13

OVERLANDING & GETTING LOCAL

After three months of living in South Africa and overcoming the initial paranoia created by the crime statistics, I felt brave enough to take a solo overnight train journey on the Shosholoza Meyl Railways from Durban to Beaufort West. I had planned to meet Andre, an *Afrikaner* friend who owned a hostel and a café in the Karoo. The train left at the expected time of 6:30 p.m. and was to reach Beaufort West the following day at 4:15 p.m. Instead, it stopped in the middle of nowhere the next morning at 8 a.m.

I strolled into the train cafeteria, expecting to find the carriage packed with passengers but found only about five others. I settled down at a breakfast table by the window with a cup of black tea and waited for my omelet and toast to arrive.

Peering through the dusty window, I saw precisely three huts close to the railway tracks, a couple of trees, and a clothesline with clothes hanging to dry. An *Ouma*† leaned against the door of one of the huts with one hand perched on her hip. She was dressed in a traditional bright yellow and blue dress with a matching yellow floral cloth wrapped around her head. The colors of her clothes complimented the desert's palette holding burnt tones of orange and brown, spiked by green in spots and meeting the stark blue of the sky in the distant horizon. She seemed to stare straight at me. But I knew she was staring at the train, perhaps a frequent occurrence for her. I wondered what she was doing here?

---

* *Afrikaner*, a Southern African ethnic group descended from Dutch settlers in the 17th and 18th centuries

† *Ouma*, South African term used to affectionately address a grandmother or elderly woman

A couple of hours later, the train had not moved an inch. Looking from the sky, the yellow, purple, and blue colored train in the vast stillness of the surrounding desert could have been a picture on a postcard. There was nothing and no one else in sight.

I felt as if we had been stranded in the wild wild west on an almost empty train. My mind conjured up an image of gangsters with rifles arriving on horses to loot the train. I pictured Clint Eastwood on a horse, a Marlboro dangling in his mouth and a gun on his hips in the distance. Before the title music of the movie "The Good, the Bad and the Ugly" began to play, I chuckled at my runaway thoughts and told myself, "Stop!"

After writing a brief message to Andre informing him about the delay, I decided to resume writing my paper on sustainable agriculture, which was due at the university in a few weeks. Some more time went by. Eventually, the train conductor, a middle-aged *Afrikaner* with a round belly matching his round glasses and a receding hairline, came by to inform us that the train was delayed!

It was about damn time!

"Why has the train stopped here?" I inquired.

"We don't know. All we know is that we don't have the signal to proceed," he replied.

"Do you know for how long?" Andre was waiting to pick me up at Beaufort West.

"Maybe a couple of more hours. Can't say," he winked and walked away.

I couldn't help but notice the contrast with rail travel in India. For one, there would be at least a few hundred passengers aboard the train. By now, the almost empty landscape would have been filled with the clamor of people arriving from neighboring villages to sell snacks, chai, coffee, samosas, and other local trinkets.

A few more hours went by. A couple of us hopped outside to get some fresh air and walk to shake out the restlessness. The *Ouma* had disappeared by now, but three children played outside the huts, oblivious to our presence. Aroused by curiosity, I began to entertain the idea of walking over to their home and solve the mystery of their existence in this deserted desert. The train conductor chose that moment to poke his head through the carriage door and holler,

"We are going to depart at any moment now. Better get back in if you don't want to be left behind."

That was the best news I had heard in a while. Relieved, I went back to my spot in the cafeteria and took in the landscape for the last time. Half an hour later, the train had still not moved. The train conductor came by and announced,

"False alarm. We are still waiting for the signal."

Unlike the German or Swiss trains renowned for seldom being late, Indian trains are often late. Consequently, I am used to train delays. But at this time, I couldn't help but feel exasperated by the lack of information.

"Oh, no! How much longer do you think this will take?"

"I hope soon. Can I join you for lunch?" asked the train conductor, "I am Ben."

The cafeteria was running out of food. I had to make do with soggy French fries and cold cheese toast, a far cry from the delicious home-made food shared by other passengers from their *dabbas** or the *thali*† from the Indian rail canteen.

"It is unusual to meet an Indian woman on a train here in South Africa," he expressed his curiosity as he slid into the chair opposite mine. It was indeed lovely to discuss and learn about South Africa's *Afrikaner* history. Rather unexpectedly and with an air of confidence, he popped the question,

"Will you marry me?"

I was dumbfounded and rendered speechless at his intrepid boldness. Was he serious? Or was he trying to lighten up my somber mood? Not knowing his true intentions, I decided that the best line of response was to deter him.

---

*   *dabbas*, a box filled with home-made food to take on a journey

†   *thali*, Indian meal made up of an assortment of various dishes to make a complete meal and served on a round platter

"I have a boyfriend."

"Can you not give him up for me?" he persisted.

"No." I was firm.

"You don't know what you are saying no to," he pressed on.

"But I know what I am saying yes to. Sorry!"

To my relief, he let it go. Once again, my mind flew to an Indian train where card games and a little festival dancing would be in full swing by now! Silence and stillness are abnormal in Indian train travel, even when stuck in the middle of nowhere. Yet, I found myself admitting that there was something evocative about being engulfed by the stillness of the vast South African desert. It was perhaps during these hours of being still that I fell in love with South Africa?

A good ten hours later, the train rolled into Beaufort West at 2 a.m.

"Are you sure you won't give him up for me?" the conductor yelled to my surprise as I jumped out of the train.

The train station was stark empty except for Andre, who was waiting by the station's dimly lit front porch. It was too late to sit back in his cactus garden and relish his famous almond croissants fresh out of the oven with a cappuccino. But I was looking forward to a good night's sleep.

* * *

Cheap domestic and regional airfares cannot replace the eternal charm and the romanticism of train travel.

It remains one of my favorite ways to travel anywhere in the world with a special place in my heart for a twenty-four-hour plus train ride in India where I can spend at least a night sleeping to the chugging rhythm of the train. Every time the train crosses a state border, a whole new world of language, smells, food, and colors emerge. I come face to face with the diversity and the chaotic beauty of India. Not to mention the exciting and intriguing encounters that could only happen on a long train journey. A book, a cup of sweet chai, and a window seat are all I need to round it all up.

When possible, travel overland. Don't even think about flying.

Overlanding is a more conscientious and sustainable way to travel. Most slow travelers will fly to their first destination. After a while, they will make their way to their next destination along the slow road. By that, I mean by bus, train, bicycling, boat, etc. The beauty of slow traveling is that we have time. There is no need to rush.

I like to say that when overlanding, my body, mind, and soul arrive together.

Trains & Buses

Booking trains and buses is relatively straightforward. Most countries will have a website for trains and the different bus companies. A word of warning, they may not be easy to navigate and may not be in English. Get help from a local friend or pull out a language translator app. Otherwise, go straight to the local train/bus station or a travel agent to buy the tickets.

Always check for deals. For example, Germany's Deutsche Bahn used to have a bundled deal on train tickets in regional sectors that let you take up to five friends for the price of one!

Seat61, the official site of "the man in sixty-one…" is an excellent resource for everything related to worldwide train travel, including links to local ticket booking websites. To find bus travel routes and worldwide prices, I like to check **Busbud**.

Journey Planning

Let's say you are in Rome, and your next destination is Rio de Janeiro in Brazil. You want to find all the possible ways to go from Rome to Rio. That's precisely what **Rome2rio** is all about. Do it now. Go to the Rome2Rio website and plug in your journey from Rome, Italy, to Rio de Janeiro, Brazil. It will show you not only the most direct way of getting from Rome to Rio (which is by plane) but also offers alternate options. These could include a mix of flight, bus, train, and ferry. Choose the route that fancies you or create a new cocktail based on what you find.

Now just for fun, try another search: Addis Ababa University, Ethiopia to Tangier, Morocco.

Google Maps is equally good at showing journey routes, but it does not work over vast geography.

Navigation

Whether you have a car, are on foot or a bicycle, until you are familiar with the local roads and directions, navigation apps are handy. We no longer see travelers peering into the city map to find that side street with the best French pastry in town. Instead, we see them with a smartphone and apps like **Google Maps**, **Waze**, and **Navmii**.

What I like about **Maps.me** is that you can use it even when offline. Download the city/country map when you are online and use it offline, even in a remote area with no or limited internet connection.

Car Rentals

As much as I prefer to travel using public transport, there are times when I have rented a car for short trips. Usually, these are times when I want to travel to areas which are difficult or inaccessible to reach by public transport. On other occasions, I rented a car when a few of us wanted to explore a region together by sharing a rental car.

Rules for car rentals are different in different countries. Here are things to consider before booking a rental car:

- Which side of the road do people drive where you are going? If you are from the U.K. and travel to the USA, it takes some practice before you get comfortable driving on the other side of the road.

- While automatic cars are a norm in the USA, most of the world uses manual cars. How confident are you with driving a manual car? If you aren't, practice a little before you get onto a highway.

- Usually, liability insurance is mandatory and included in the rental car price, but collision damage might not be. Does your credit card cover collision damage in the country where you are going? If not, buy it through the rental car agency. Collision damage can also be added as an option to your travel insurance policy.

- Inquire about getting roadside assistance just in case you get stuck somewhere with a flat tire or run out of gas on a dirt road miles away from civilization.

- Always pay by credit card for car rentals. You can dispute the charge later if you find any errors in the final bill or if the rental car company adds suspicious amounts initially not agreed upon.

- Watch out for other costs like VAT road tax, eco-tax, etc., that get tacked onto the base rental price and increase the total rent.

- Get familiar with the local road signs and road etiquette. It is rude to honk in the USA, but it is a norm in some countries like India and Indonesia. Even if you don't honk, be ready to hear a symphony of honks around you and stay calm!

Forget-me-not:
Remember to collect miles if the rental car company is a partner with your frequent flyer program.

I have usually found good rental car deals with **Expedia**, a rental car aggregator. As with flights, always compare the prices with other aggregators like **Rentalcars** and **Kayak**.

Automatic cars cost more than manual ones in most countries.

Monthly rentals will cost less than weekly rentals. Weekly rentals will cost less than for a partial week. Plan accordingly and save.

The Conscious Slow Traveler

#1 Choose carpooling services and be even more eco-friendly.

Use services like **Poparide** in Canada, for instance, for in-country or regional transportation. These are the Airbnb of overlanding. If someone has a car and is going from A to B with empty seats in their car, they are willing to take others with them for a small cost. In short, you carpool with others to your destination. This type of carpooling service is not available everywhere, but it is worth checking to see if it is.

Search on the internet for *"rideshares <country name>"* in the local language, and it will pop-up the popular ridesharing services. For instance, in Germany, search for *"Mitfahrgelegenheit Deutschland"* and *"rideshare Danemark"* in Denmark to get more accurate results. **Blablacar** is the world's leading and trusted long-distance carpooling platform.

#2 Go local.

When booking rental cars, choose to rent from local companies and put your money into the pocket of a local business and not that of multinational chains like Hertz, Avis, Budget, etc. But here is the catch: Big rental car companies tend to offer cheaper rates, and they will most likely accept your credit card's collision damage coverage, saving you a lot of money. Local car companies, most likely, will not accept your credit card's coverage, and their rental cost may be slightly higher, thus driving up the total price.

At this point, a dilemma arises—whether to go with a big rental car company and save a bunch or go with a local car rental company and pay more but stay true to the conscious slow traveler mantra?

We often fall into such quandaries when walking the path of a conscious slow traveler. I don't have a black and white answer to such a predicament. The answer will depend on your unique circumstances. The best way to resolve this is by checking in with your inner compass.

When booking tours or guides, don't book with tourism companies from your home country. These will most certainly cost you more. Once on the ground, scout for local tour companies and guides that directly profit the local communities.

#3 Adopt a car-free lifestyle.

It is almost impossible in the USA to live without a car unless you spend all your time in a place like New York City, which has excellent inner-city public transport. Luckily, in most parts of the world, public transportation is readily available.

Adopt a car-free lifestyle when you can and save a bundle on auto insurance and fuel. Try to make the most of the local buses, trains, shared vans, shared taxis, *tuk-tuks** and such for your everyday needs like the locals do. In Sayulita, Mexico, people use golf carts to get around the little town!

Walk or cycle when you can. You will not only stay healthy and befriend the locals along the way, but there's a lot you will see and sense when not on four wheels. Most of all, the slowness of walking or bicycling will sensitize you to the subtle changes and nuances in the scene around you, which would otherwise get lost when zooming by.

#4 Don't fall for the buzzwords.

Green, Eco, Sustainable, and Fair Trade have become buzzwords that play on our desire to leave a lower footprint on the planet. These words compel us to rethink our choices. Rightly so. The flip-side is that agencies and companies use them as catchphrases in marketing their services or products to capitalize on our desire to be more responsible. They are not always or necessarily green, eco, sustainable, or fair trade as advertised.

Please don't book a tour because it is advertised as being eco-friendly. A product may not be organic simply because it is labeled organic. A store that says fair trade might not be paying their workers as they claim to be. Spend some time on the ground to acclimatize with the local scene. You will find the genuine ones.

---

*   *tuk-tuks*, three-wheeled taxi on a motorcycle commonly used in Asia and Africa for cheap public transportation, also called rickshaws

Resources

	App	Website	Cost
Trains		seat61.com	Free
Car rentals	Expedia Rentalcars.com KAYAK	expedia.com rentalcars.com kayak.com	Free
Navigation & GPS	Google Maps Waze Navigation & Live Traffic Navmii MAPS.ME	maps.google.com waze.com navmii.com maps.me	Free
Journey planning	Rome2Rio: Trip Planner	rome2rio.com	Free
Bus planning	Busbud	busbud.com	Free
Carpooling	BlaBlaCar: Carpooling and Bus	blablacar.com	Free

Chapter 14

Traveling to Places Where You Don't Know the Local Lingo?

*H*ola! Hej! Ciao! Bonjour! Molo! Aloha! Hello! Silav!

It feels good to be greeted in your tongue by a foreigner, doesn't it?

Just a few words of the local lingo work like magic. They open up portals of warmth in people's hearts, even with a few words at the risk of sounding foolish.

They might even laugh or giggle at your accent or your struggle to get the right guttural sound. But they will appreciate your attempt, and it will boost your self-confidence. Immediately, a sense of kinship and a bond develops. Don't be surprised if you get invited for dinner by people you have just met and get access to adventures beyond the tourist track.

Someone once told me that the best way to break cultural barriers is to learn some commonly used swear words. Ahem! I won't suggest you go that far—unless you have a penchant for swear words, and you are sure your audience will appreciate them.

Speaking a few words shows respect for the local lingo. Moreover, language is a way to experience a new culture as you would through its food, music, colors, clothes, history, and traditions. By knowing the local language, you can also appreciate a culture's humor. It is undoubtedly useful if you decide to venture off the beaten track into areas where the only way to communicate might be the local language and some gestures.

Did I mention romance? What if you like someone who does not speak your language? Learning theirs could be a beginning and can give you an excellent excuse to meet up!

Apart from making your travels go smoother, more interesting, and possibly romantic or adventurous, learning a new language exercises your brain. It challenges you to concentrate, improves memory, and increases attention span. Scientists now know that brain development continues while you are learning as you are growing new synaptic connections. One study by Toronto's Baycrest Health Sciences has revealed that learning a new language delays the onset of Alzheimer's disease and dementia by four to five years.

Experimenting with new words, phrases, and slangs boost creativity and divergent thinking. The American Academy of Neurology has performed studies showing that speaking more than one language increases the brain's neural pathways, allowing information to be processed through a greater variety of channels.

Here is an example of how this process works in everyday life. Let's say you need to get your clothes to the laundry. You have located the closest one on Google maps, and you walk there with your sack bursting to the seams with clothes. When you arrive, you find that the laundry is closed because it is Monday. So, you stop a local passing by intending to ask, "Is there another laundry nearby? This one is closed." You had learned the word for laundry yesterday, but at this moment, when you need it, "laundry" in the local tongue becomes like an elusive mistress. You draw a blank.

Automatically, your brain switches gears into the problem-solving mode and begins to think of other ways to explain what you want to ask. Not just by using different words, but also through miming the action of washing. You might point to the sack of clothes and use other words like "water" or "soap" with a scrubbing motion to indicate washing. Your brain's goal is to get across the term "laundry" to the passerby. And it kick-starts its creative, problem-solving, and divergent thinking functions.

 Moreover, food tastes better when ordered in the local language!

Vineeth, a fellow traveler and author who has recently published a book, said:

"...to learn a few sentences in the local language (proverbs), some research into local music, movie culture, and cuisine, favorite celebrity or idols of the locals, and some fun facts. Things like this tend to bring me in close contact with the locals. Nothing is overwhelming in travel, then being able to crack that joke with the locals that they accept you as one of their own."

6 Ways to Learn the Local Lingo Without Breaking Your Budget

#1 Enroll in a language school.

The first time I enrolled in a Spanish language school was in Quetzaltenango, Guatemala, in 2003. What I loved about the school was that there was an emphasis on conversational Spanish. We did learn about verbs and conjugating verbs. But the school did not drown us by making us learn grammar. I know I would not have survived for two weeks had they headed in that direction.

Language schools provide a wonderful opportunity to meet other travelers and locals. You might even meet a local who wants to learn your language. It could be the beginning of a language exchange partnership over a beer or two, leading to a friendship.

Here are some ways to begin your search for language schools in the country you are going to.

- Search for *"<language> language schools in <city/country name>"* on the internet.
- Consult the local tourist information office.
- Ask on the local expat Facebook group.
- Check at the local library.
- Read flyers in places frequented by travelers such as cafes, restaurants, and hostels.
- Ask your host/landlord.

While it is easy to find affordable language schools in Latin America, that may not be the case everywhere. That's when language learning apps can come to your rescue.

#2 Use language learning apps.

These apps are perfect for learners that prefer to study at their own pace versus in a classroom or when language learning schools don't exist. Some apps have an online community as well as a native speaker that you can chat with, making this learning experience semi-real.

What makes using these apps interesting is that they gamify the learning process making language learning fun! They are easy to use, and with just a few minutes of practice every day, you will be surprised how much you will learn. Utilize those extra minutes while waiting for the bus from Arequipa to Cusco or that long flight from London to Kyoto and get a head-start on the language.

I like **Duolingo** and **Babbel. Memrise, HelloTalk, Tripling,** and **HiNative** are other popular language learning apps.

#3 Replace classroom learning with real-life learning.

My next venture into Spanish learning was in 2016 in Peru. Josip, a native Andean and a student who loved playing flute, had posted his teaching services for a very reasonable price in the Cusco expat group on Facebook. He was looking to make some money to fund part of his college fees. A brief chat at The Meeting Point café in the San Blas neighborhood in Cusco later, I decided to hire him for one-on-one lessons.

After the first two classes, we strolled down from the San Blas neighborhood towards the San Pedro market. On the way, there were many cafes, souvenir shops, restaurants, and tourists. With the help of Josip, I learned to have an ordinary conversation about what we saw, the colors, and the souvenirs for sale. I learned how to bargain, ask for the ingredients in a local dish, and explain that I am vegetarian. Discovering the names for the local fruits, vegetables, herbs, and cheese in the San Pedro market and trying to pronounce them while having a conversation with the vendors turned into a playful adventure.

As travelers, what we need on the road is to have simple conversations to navigate everyday life.

Where is the bus station? How much does this cost? Would you like to go for a coffee with me? It is not crucial to learn how to conjugate "to drive" in the past perfect tense!

#4 Take part in a language immersion program.

These are a step up from language schools. Immersion programs include a homestay with a local family besides the classroom learning, like the one I had signed up for in Guatemala. You live with a family for a few weeks and practice speaking their language daily. You get involved with their day-to-day life, interactions with each other and with their friends and family, colleagues, and neighbors in an authentic way.

I learned to make tamales from my host family in Guatemala. I also learned that they had lost family during the Guatemalan genocide of the Mayan people during the 1980s. The school I had enrolled in was a non-profit whose intention was to search and bring back the Mayans who had escaped the genocide, reunite them with their families, and resettle them into new communities in Guatemala again.

Immersion may be an intense experience for some, especially if your own culture and lifestyle are dramatically different. A high degree of openness and adaptability is required, even if it is for a short time. If the idea of an immersion feels too intense, start with enrolling in a language school and then take a step towards immersion. Or start with a short immersion period to test the waters and get comfortable.

Take a look at **Lingoo** to find language immersion programs in the country of your choice.

#5 Use online language translators.

These are very useful when you want to translate information. Such as about a course you are interested in or when someone sends you an email with information about a tour you want to go on, or when you are reading local news online.

The most commonly used tools for language translation on-the-go are **Google Translate** or **BabelFish**. They are easy to use, and you can translate from one language to another without learning even an iota of the new language.

#6 Use everyday tools to go further down the lingo learning rabbit hole.

Pretend to be a kid and watch movies and TV series in the local lingo meant for them. Head to the local library to borrow children's books. Listen to local music. Use everyday resources for learning further like **Youtube, Spotify, Pandora**, and **Netflix**.

If you are going to stay for a longer time, then it's well worth the effort to go deeper into the lingo rabbit hole.

And Finally, Practice

No matter how many courses you take and how many apps you use, if you don't get out there and practice speaking, you will not learn!

Challenge yourself to speak at least a few words in the local language each day. Try not to speak in your mother tongue or English at all. Once you know the basics, you will be surprised at how fast you will pick up the accent and the rhythm by listening to the local people in their natural environment such as markets, cafes, bus stations, etc.

Can We Avoid Language Faux Pas?

At times, the same word in the same language, but a different country can have a completely different meaning. Here is an example. In Mexican Spanish, *coger* is a slang word for "to fuck." In Puerto Rican Spanish, *coger* means "to take" or "to catch" as in "take the bus" or "catch the bus."

Imagine...

You are waiting at a bus stop in Mexico and don't know which bus to take to go to the local market. You decide to practice your language skills and ask a Mexican standing next to you,

"Which bus can I take to go to the market?"

You use the verb *coger* because that's what you learned in Puerto Rico.

"¿Qué autobus puedo coger para ir al mercado?"

You get ugly stares or giggles from people nearby instead of an answer. And you wonder why?!

Can we avoid language faux pas?

Not completely. Not until you master the language, its slang, and local usage. Until then, be willing to be laughed at and laugh at yourself. Apologize sincerely. Use a language translator app to convey what you wanted to say when in need.

Everyday Words & Phrases to Get Started With

Hello, Thank you, Sorry, Excuse me	Good morning/ afternoon/eve-ning /night	I don't speak <local language>	Do you speak English?
What is your name?	My name is <your name>	I am from <country>	Where are you from?
I didn't under-stand what you said.	Where is the bus/train station?	Where can I buy the tickets?	How much does this cost?
It is hot/cold/ foggy/ rainy/ humid/cloudy.	Here, there, this, that	And, or, what, which, why, how much, who	Restaurant, local market, supermarket
Doctor, dentist, hospital, pharmacy, emergency	Police, police station	Mother, father, man, woman, boy, girl	North, south, east, west
Calendar months (January to December)	Numbers (1 to 10)	Days of the week (Monday to Sunday)	

Resources

	App	Website	Cost
Language immersion		lingoo.com	Free
Language translators	Google Translate	translate.google.com babelfish.com	Free
Language learning apps	Duolingo Babbel Memrise HelloTalk HINative		Free

CHAPTER 15

AVOIDING CULTURAL FAUX PAS: CULTURAL INTELLIGENCE

FEBRUARY 2020 - SAN JUAN CHAMULA, MEXICO

"Chamula is a fiercely independent and autonomous indigenous community. They don't follow the Mexican government's laws but their own," Alex, our local guide, informed us.

"So be careful if you decide to come here on your own," he warned us.

It was the day of the carnival. The people of Chamula were dressed in traditional clothing and took part in colorful parades and beautiful ancestral dances. The community leaders led healing rituals and chants in incense-filled rooms decorated with maize, pine needles, and various depictions of deities from the Christian and Mayan faiths.

"In this community, Catholicism is interwoven with old Mayan tradition. The annual festivals reflect this strongly," Alex educated us.

He then led us to the house of one of the community leaders of Chamula. The leader, who was visibly drunk, welcomed us and offered us many rounds of homemade *posh**.

Later, we strolled into the church of San Juan Chamula. Alex asked us to put our cameras away in our bags.

"The people of Chamula are very private. They do not tolerate anyone taking pictures of them or their places of worship. They are very serious about this," Alex informed us with a solemn look on his face.

---

*   *posh*, a local alcoholic beverage made from sugarcane and an integral part of the festivities

Entering the church was like stepping through a portal into another dimension. On the pine needle carpet, people kneeled and chanted prayers in front of a sea of curiously arranged candles, chicken sacrifices, eggs, and bones, all in a mist of the sharp scent of incense. It was apparent how Catholicism had been woven into the fabric of the Mayan faith.

"We'll stay on this side and quietly observe so as not to interfere or disturb the locals while they perform their rituals," Alex guided us.

An American couple from our group stood with their arms around each other in a gentle embrace, observing the scene before them respectfully. In a different context, this would be rather normal, wouldn't it? But not in Chamula. Soon enough, a local man walked up to them. He shook his head and waved his finger at them disapprovingly while saying something in *Tzotzil**.

"He is telling you that you cannot hug each other inside the church or anywhere in public in Chamula," Alex translated for us.

It doesn't matter what we think is right or wrong. It's about respecting traditions, culture, and what is okay for the local people.

* * *

In our everyday lives, we assume that the world appears, behaves, communicates, and relates in the same way we are accustomed to. Yet this is far from the truth. Marijntje, the "little mother of the river Rhine" who I met in 2017 at the Writer's Group in Cusco, recounted her time in Shanghai.

> *"When my neighbor finally visited me after four months, she brought her own thermos with coffee, her own mug, and biscuits."*

Hand, eye, facial, and body gestures can have vastly different meanings in different countries and cultures. How you sit or greet someone, or even the extent to which you reach out and touch someone, can be interpreted in unexpected ways. Disengaging with the local ways takes away part of the magic of experiencing something different, robbing us of the opportunity to grow beyond our known comfortable ways.

---

* *Tzotzil*, Maya language spoken by the indigenous Tzotzil Maya people in Chiapas, Mexico

Common Cultural Faux Pas

Because each culture varies so much that what is acceptable in one could be taboo in another, the best way to find out about the local cultural norms is to ask other travelers, locals, and expats. Research the cultural norms of the place you are going to and adapt accordingly. In this section, I have listed some common faux pas that travelers experience.

Religious sites, festivals, rituals, and ceremonies

Places of worship, festivals, ceremonies, and rituals hold profound religious and cultural significance for the believers of that faith. It is important to remember that we are visitors, even if we are staying long-term.

In Ubud, I was not allowed to enter the Pura Gunung Lebah temple because I was wearing a sleeveless top and shorts. In India and Bali, menstruating women are not allowed into temples, and shoes must be removed before entering.

Suppose that a local person invites you to rituals and ceremonies that are so sacred that they are off-limits for foreigners and tourists. It indicates that the person inviting you has developed a level of trust with you and wants to share something significant from their culture. These experiences are often mind-blowing and can be transformative. On these occasions, observe and take part without judgment—even if it challenges your own beliefs.

Lastly, don't convert this privilege into a spectacle to be posted on social media. Always be ready to apologize if you err.

Body language/usage

In many Muslim countries and India, eating with the left hand is considered offensive. The left hand is reserved for a dirty use (ahem!) and thus not considered fit for eating.

Sitting with your feet pointed at a saint, temple/shrine, or an elderly person is deemed disrespectful in Southeast Asia.

Greetings

Greeting a woman by kissing on the cheeks is a standard way of greeting in Spain, Italy, Latin America, and France, but would make someone extremely uncomfortable in the USA, Asia, and some parts of Europe. It will likely get you into trouble in the Middle East. In the USA and many parts of Europe, it is customary to shake hands to greet. In Japan, the traditional way of greeting is to bow.

Eye contact

In the USA and Western Europe, making eye contact with the opposite gender indicates interest. It can be flirtatious depending on the context. If you don't return the eye contact, you show that you are not interested, are distracted, or lack confidence. But in Japan if a Japanese woman avoids making eye contact, it does not imply a lack of interest or self-confidence. She is only being polite and respectful according to her culture.

Dress code

Be mindful of what you wear and follow the local rules.

In India, women wearing skin-revealing clothes in public could attract unwanted attention. You could be subjected to lewd behavior, catcalling, eve-teasing, or being humiliated in public. It varies from region to region within India, but to dress on the side of modesty will keep you safe, no matter where.

The concept of time

In India, when a gathering is planned for 6 p.m, the hosts expect the guests to arrive after 7 p.m.

They will find it strange if the guests show up promptly on time. They may not even be ready to receive the timely guests! Being late is entirely normal. In contrast, in Germany, if you are invited for dinner or have an appointment with a German, be on time. Being late is considered rude. This punctuality is also reflected by the German trains. They are seldom late.

Tipping

One of the follies of travel is not leaving a tip where you are expected to and leaving one where you are not. In some countries, people count on tips to make their income, such as in India or Mexico. To contrast, some countries such as Iceland are no-tipping countries.

How does one know whether to tip or not?

Ask other travelers, locals, and post questions in the local expat group on Facebook.

I follow a general rule of thumb that works everywhere: Tip between 10% and 15%.

Bargaining

In some countries, bargaining is the norm—a game that the seller expects the buyer to play. It is part of the culture. The price tag is only a way to initiate banter with the buyer before reaching a compromise. Sometimes, the seller will jack up the price right from the beginning, hoping that if you don't bargain, they can make a few more dollars.

I am not suggesting that you must bargain, but do. Don't feel awkward about bargaining in countries where it is part of the culture. If you are not used to it in your home country, then don't be shy. Give it a shot and take it as a fun adventure even if you might end up paying more for an item than a local would have. Most importantly, enjoy this game of haggling.

Bargaining in general is possible in places like local markets, flea markets, and souvenir shops, but not malls, supermarkets, upscale shops, or boutiques. (Walk into a five-star Sheraton, ask for a room price, and then try to bargain it down—I don't think so.)

How Can I Avoid Cultural Faux Pas?

You can't. We can't. Not completely.

We are humans, and we don't know everything. As much as we

might prepare, we are still prone to making innocent mistakes. Cultural faux pas are usually silly, laughable, and often made out of ignorance. That's okay. More often than not, locals are tolerant and accepting. If they know that you mean well by your actions and that you are trying to understand their cultural norms, they may open up to you and help you—and perhaps even give you insights into their lives. Moreover, respect often fosters respect in return.

Stay open to being corrected as you might be warned for your behavior or appearance. Accept it respectfully and follow the advice. I adhere to this three-point axiom:

Observe. Ask. Follow.

A few faux pas later, you will start to unlock the intriguing mysteries of the new culture you find yourself in.

The Conscious Slow Traveler

#1 Be gracious when bargaining.

Know that the vendors also have to earn a living. Don't drive the price down too hard, especially if you have a currency advantage. Be kind and don't bargain simply for the fun of it when you have no intention of buying anything at all.

#2 Don't tip more than the norm.

If you are traveling to countries where you get a currency advantage, don't tip beyond the norm just because "It's so cheap!" be it in restaurants, tour guides, taxi drivers, or agents. I have seen this happen many times in different countries.

To illustrate this point, I will use this example. In Cusco, because things are relatively cheaper, sometimes travelers tend to tip extravagantly beyond the norm. This behavior creates a subtle shift in the minds of the locals. It is even more disruptive for small service providers, like taxis. If three *soles* for a taxi ride in the inner city of Cusco feels inexpensive and you give the driver ten *soles* instead (because of your generous spirit), over time, the taxi drivers learn to charge travelers ten *soles* and not three.

Moreover, taxi drivers may start refusing locals because they can earn more from foreigners. Sooner or later, the locals begin harboring resentment toward travelers and a disruption in the local economy—albeit subtle—begins. A few years down the line, travelers may complain that Cuscanian taxi drivers have a different price for foreigners and locals. It is not fair! But remember, it takes two to tango.

CHAPTER 16

DIGITALLY SAVVY, BUT MINIMAL

Digital minimalism is a philosophy that helps you question what digital communication tools (and behaviors surrounding these tools) add the most value to your life. It is motivated by the belief that intentionally and aggressively clearing away low-value digital noise, and optimizing your use of the tools that really matter, can significantly improve your life.

Cal Newport, a computer science professor at Georgetown University and author of the book Digital Minimalism: Choosing a Focused Life in a Noisy World

Since the early 2000s, the world has gone through a digital revolution. The internet is now available in all parts of the world and has permeated all sections of society. Information at your fingertips is the new paradigm. With that, my well-stacked rows of Lonely Planet guidebooks on my bookshelf tiptoed their way into storage boxes. Apps on my iPhone and bookmarked links on my MacBook Pro became the new digital guidebooks.

In this technology obsessed age, I suspect that we have all gone digital a step too far. Or am I old-fashioned? Didn't we enjoy a coffee in a cafe and start a conversation with someone new? Instead, now we hide behind the screens of our laptops or phones, inundated with messages, notifications, social media, and information overload. We ignore the people around us to cyber-connect with people on the other side of the world.

We consume information spewed on the internet, becoming obsessed with the news, messages, texts, emails, videos, tweeting, Facebooking, and Instagramming.

In short, we are living in an age of digital overdose.

How About a Digital Diet?

An analysis published by the Computers in Human Behavior journal has concluded that:

> *People who report using seven to eleven social media platforms have more than three times the risk of depression and anxiety than their peers who use zero to two platforms, even after adjusting for the total time spent on social media overall.*

To be honest, we cannot be efficient without the internet. The internet is a powerful source for a plethora of useful, relevant, and timely information. So, I dare not propose going back to the digitally nonexistent days. In the age of food diets, I suggest a digital diet. In this diet, we consciously choose what information we savor, not gorge, when, and how often. Following this diet means being digitally savvy but minimal.

 It urges an addiction to real life and not to digital life.

It's a good idea to remind yourself that you are slow traveling to experience the world with all your senses and not the World Wide Web from behind a screen. Running into strangers, starting spontaneous conversations, and discovering things through them still holds an old-world charm—much like reading from a good old-fashioned book made of actual paper instead of reading on an e-reader. It is good to remind ourselves that the world still went around when there was no internet and we relied on our social and navigational skills to find our way around.

Moreover, when our mind is free from information overload, we tend to slow down. We are no longer anxious to tick off a bucket list of things to do and see in this new place that we discovered on the internet. Isn't that the point of slow traveling after all—to slow down, not only our physical pace but also our mental pace?

You won't truly enjoy your love affair tied to your smartphone or other digital devices. So, edit your digital life often and mercilessly. After all, it is your masterpiece.

7 Tips for a Digital Diet

#1 Learn what you need and unglue yourself.

Don't overwhelm yourself with information about something that you will need three months from now. Search and bookmark the pages and websites you find interesting to look at later for more details. Put reminders on your phone to look up information a few days before you think you might need it.

Take notes using apps like **EverNote** that you can refer to later. Use apps like **Pocket** to save content (not only travel-related) that you can access and read later.

#2 Allow room for spontaneity.

Search for enough information, but don't overdo it. Allow things to reveal themselves at the museum, on the walking tour, in the local market, through other fellow slow travelers or locals you meet, etc.

#3 Avoid local SIM cards with data.

If you decide to get a local SIM card, opt only to call, text, and drop the data option. That may be difficult these days because call, text, and data come bundled together. If that is the case, get the lowest data pack possible and reserve it for emergency usage. This way you will resist the temptation to look at your social media or surf the internet while waiting for your food in a restaurant!

Not having continual access to the internet will free up your mind and attention to breathe in the local smells, take in the sights, and simply hang out in the **Now**. Perhaps push yourself out of your comfort zone and start a conversation with another person while waiting for the bus at the bus stop? Or conjure up a poem.

#4 Unplug entirely for 24 hours once a week.

You will be blown away by how much free time you have! You will confront life straight on in its everyday ordinariness without the dulling mediation of a screen. This time "off" will allow you to discover which activities and behaviors are precious for you in your life and which are merely mindless distractions.

#5 Keep human interactions, kill the non-human ones.

Turn off notifications, badges, and sounds for apps on your phone. It will cut down the amount of buzzing and reduce addiction to these apps. Declutter your email inbox from those unnecessary and irrelevant newsletters and subscriptions that you signed up for voluntarily or involuntarily. Delete the apps that don't add any value to your life.

But keep the messages and notifications coming from real people.

#6 Cultivate everyday discipline not to spend more than X hours in the digital space.

Get the necessary done within a fixed window of time. As soon as you restrict your online time, you will notice that you become more efficient and waste less time on casual browsing, checking updates, reading news, etc.

#7 Get out without any digital device.

Once you become familiar with the new place you are in and your neighborhood, venture out for a stroll or a bus ride without any digital devices. That includes your smartphone. It is freeing!

 It's all about finding that sweet spot between being digitally savvy, but minimal.

Isn't it?

CHAPTER 17

FOOD & HEALTH

OCTOBER 2009 - MILAN, ITALY

6:30 p.m.

I stood in front of a restaurant on Via Marghera that was recommended by Antonio, my colleague.

"They have the best pizza in that area with real *mozzarella di bufala*," he had told me earlier that day.

I was salivating at the image of slightly melted blobs of fresh *mozzarella di bufala* on a perfectly baked pizza crust with an otherworldly tasting tomato sauce. Crispy at the first bite yet light and fluffy on the inside, piled with fresh arugula leaves and a few cloves of roasted garlic.

"Why do the tomatoes taste so extraordinarily delicious here in Italy?" I had asked Antonio on a different occasion during a work trip to Pisa.

"I think you have not been eating real tomatoes until now! Welcome to Italy, the land of *la dolce vita!*" He had replied, gesticulating with his hands as only the Italians do.

"*Buona serata, signora*. We are not open for dinner before 8 p.m, but you can enjoy our *aperitivos**," the restaurant manager informed me.

What? Not open for dinner until 8 p.m?

To my agony, I discovered that this is the norm for most restaurants in *Milano†*. All I could get between 6 p.m. and 8 p.m. to satisfy my hunger pangs were *aperitivos*. Or survive on a slice of pizza or

---

* *aperitivos*, buffet of unlimited bite-sized starters and a drink

† *Milano*, the Italian name for the city of Milan. After having lived there for eighteen months, saying Milan feels very odd to my tongue! As a way of expressing my affections for this city, I have taken the liberty of referring to it as Milano in this anecdote

a panini from the take-out pizzerias.

This kicked my apartment hunting into overdrive. Within a month of arriving in *Milano*, I had settled into a classic Milanese apartment on the fourth floor with a terrace overlooking the rooftops of the picturesque city. And a kitchen.

Soon I developed a routine: Saturday morning open-air farmer's market on Viale Papiniano for fresh produce, NatureSi on Via Cesare Correnti for organic health food, and India Shop Milano near Porto Venezia for all things Indian.

Be Bop in Navigli became my hotspot for mouthwatering pizza and sensual *tiramisu*. Beato Te in the Bisceglie area, close to work, worked for lunchtime pizza and calzones. Rangoli in La Brera satiated the Indian in me.

While the heavy lifters like the puttanesca and carbonara reigned supreme over the *Milano* restaurant menu scene, I gave my heart to the little known *pizzoccheri** —an accidental discovery during a weekend trip to Tirano. A box of *pizzoccheri* pasta—yes, it's pasta and not a pizza—was available at Esselunga, the local supermarket, for 99c. But how do I cook it? YouTube videos weren't of much help for this little-known culinary delight.

I expressed my dilemma and desire to my colleague, Paula, during a morning espresso break in the office cafeteria.

"Oh, don't worry! My husband, Juliano, can show you! His family is from the Valtellina region," she came to my rescue.

"I spoke with my husband. Would you like to come sailing with us on our boat, and in the evening, he will show you how to make *pizzoccheri*?" came her offer the next day during lunch.

Sailing on Lake Maggiore, followed by pizzoccheri? How could I say no?

I offered to bring wine.

We spent the day sailing around Lake Maggiore with conversations replete with Italian politics, love, the *Milano* fashion scene, and the ritzy, glitzy elites of Italy. As the sun began to paint the

---

* *pizzoccheri*, a hearty specialty of short tagliatelle, a flat ribbon pasta made of buckwheat from the Valtellina region of Northern Italy

evening sky, Juliano set to his art of making *pizzoccheri* in the tiny but well-equipped kitchen aboard their boat. I followed him with eager eyes and ears, clutching a pen and a book in my hands, ready to take notes and not miss anything.

Pizzoccheri pasta, Valtellina casera, Bitto cheese, potatoes, savoy cabbage, and mangold leaves came together perfectly in harmony with generous dollops of butter and cloves of lightly roasted garlic. The result? Italian perfection on a plate. Paula had set up a table with a red and white checked table cloth on the upper deck. Moored on the gently bobbing shores of Lake Maggiore, *pizzoccheri* pasta paired with a glass of Tommasi Amarone Della Valpolicella was the perfect end to a perfect day.

We cemented a lifelong friendship over *pizzoccheri*. I knew that a box of *pizzoccheri* pasta was only an email to Paula away.

Eighteen months later, I left the land of *la dolce vita*. I had gained a few extra pounds.

* * *

Health is wealth.

While this is true at all times, it is even more so while on the road. We are in an alien environment. What is available in the market could be different than our food habits. Having dietary restrictions and food sensitivities could pose an additional challenge. The last thing you want is to get a *Delhi belly* or a *Bali belly** and be bedridden for days.

Take some necessary hygiene precautions, drink plenty of clean water, have some home remedies available, and keep a doctor's number handy. Keeping your gut tuned with natural probiotics such as yoghurt, kombucha, other fermented foods, or with a supplement version from the pharmacy will keep many ailments away.

Clean Water

Water is life, and it is also one of the most common reasons for

---

* *Delhi belly or Bali belly*, traveler's diarrhea caused due to an infection of the stomach and intestines. Not confined to the Indian subcontinent or Bali

travelers falling ill. The source of clean drinking water differs from country to country. In most European countries, it's safe to drink tap water. In India, you can drink tap water when provided by the municipal corporation, but boil it if it comes from a well. Nowhere in Mexico and Indonesia can you drink from the tap. When tap water is unsafe to drink, use filtered water to brush your teeth, and keep your mouth closed while showering—the easiest places to slip.

Some travelers carry water purifiers with them.

Amy, the editor of this book who now lives in Kyoto, Japan, gave her tip.

> *"I use iodine when traveling in South East Asia. Good for killing pathogens in freshwater. It's an old-school tip I learned from my father's backpacking days."*

Glen, the handyman from Denver, carries a camping UV water treatment pen. Do an internet search for *"too many adapters best water purifiers travel,"* and you will get some top recommendations for water purifiers.

How do we find out about the local drinking water situation?

Ask your landlord or post in the local expat Facebook group! You will get the answer pronto.

Self-catering

After being away from home for a while, a time comes when we crave a simple home-made meal that feels homey and cozy. Oatmeal with raisins, cinnamon, milk, and honey with a cup of coffee for breakfast. Soup for dinner. A bowl of spaghetti with the good old tomato sauce.

Having an apartment with a kitchen where you can cook even a simple meal is very useful for slow travelers. Here are some reasons.

- By cooking many of your meals, you will save money.
- If you have dietary restrictions as I do, you will be able to maintain them.

- You will have more control over hygiene and what you put in your body.

- If you are in an area with few eateries and restaurants, you will not go hungry or be malnourished.

Local Markets

Local markets are the first thing to locate in a new place. John, the taco raconteur from Bainbridge Island, says:

"The best non-people thing about any country is the big central food markets—the kind with hundreds of stalls. I always make a listing of when they are open and plan my visits around that."

Ditto!

I am a big fan of buying from local vendors and farmers. Can a supermarket beat the hustle and bustle of small shops selling locally produced food, drink, meat, herbs, grains, flowers, and dairy? Wandering in these narrow alleys is in itself a cultural and sensual explosion of sight, smell, and sound. It might just tickle you to try that frothy exotic looking drink, which the locals seem to gulp down with gusto!

Make a trip to a supermarket for things that you cannot find in these local markets and that your taste buds crave for.

Health Food Stores & Care Packages

We, the travelers, arrive in a new place with a wide array of requirements to meet our dietary and health needs. To cater to these needs, health food and organics stores have mushroomed in regions that fall on the traveler roadmap. Many slow travelers and even locals are willing to pay the price for products such as quinoa, organic basmati rice, maca powder, etc., which may not be part of the local cuisine.

When you can't find what you need or crave for locally, **Amazon** comes to the rescue to order online. There may be local versions like **FlipKart** in India and **MercadoLibre** in Latin America. Or maybe your friends and family can ship you a care package?

Sometimes other expat/slow travelers who are returning can squeeze a little something in their luggage for you.

Handling Dietary Restrictions

"Do you have anything vegetarian on the menu?"

Waiter: "Yes, we have fish."

How many times have I encountered this situation? Vegetarianism, and up to a certain extent veganism, are no longer alien concepts. I no longer get strange looks when I say I am vegetarian. But the understanding of what vegetarianism means can vary. The dish may be entirely vegetarian but could be cooked in chicken broth or duck fat. The gap between how strict a vegetarian you are and how loose is the definition of vegetarianism for the restaurant will decide what can slide into your stomach.

More stringent dietary restrictions such as being a vegetarian who is lactose and gluten intolerant, cannot eat nightshades, and has nut sensitivities are harder to manage. Adhering to a specific diet, such as Keto or Paleo, can be trickier.

DON'T let this obstacle stop you from going because you can easily overcome it in five simple ways.

#1 Get an apartment with a kitchen. You will have <u>full</u> control over your diet.

#2 Bring any necessary supplements, medications, etc. specific to your diet with you from home to last for a couple of months until you can find a local source.

#3 Identify online stores from where you can order in case local sources are not available.

#4 Can a family member or friend send you a quota that will last you for the duration of your trip?

#5 Never feel awkward or shy to ask what goes in a dish at a restaurant. Explain to them that you have health concerns or follow a diet. I have found that most often than not, restaurant owners are willing to adjust the dish to fit my requirements if the request is easy enough. During my time working in Helsinki, a few nouveau cuisine restaurants even cooked up an entirely new and extraordinarily delicious vegetarian dish for me. My dietary restrictions challenged the chef's creativity, and they raised to the occasion brilliantly. Don't hesitate to ask.

HappyCow, **Yelp,** and **TripAdvisor** are useful resources to locate restaurants that offer vegetarian, vegan, and gluten-free food options.

Eating Out on a Budget

Mom-and pop style

Some of the most delicious and budget-friendly food I have eaten while traveling has been in small mom-and-pop or "hole in the wall" style places that may not even show up in online searches. You will come across these by hitting the pavement or word-of-mouth from other slow travelers, expats, and locals. The longer you stay in a place, the higher the chance to discover these hidden local gems.

Jose, a local muralist and artist I met in Oaxaca city, took me to a restaurant in one of the side alleys, primarily frequented by the locals. What was unique about this restaurant was that a sixty *peso mezcal** order came with a three-course meal, including a dessert! You don't pay for the meal; you pay for the *mezcal*. Each time you ask for another glass of *mezcal*, you get a new three-course meal round for free! If it were not for Jose, I would have never discovered that restaurant.

Discovering these hidden and unique local places is one of the things that make slow traveling worthwhile.

---

*   *mezcal,* a traditional Mexican spirit made from oven-cooked agave

Street food

Street food is something NOT to be missed when slow traveling. It is the heart and soul of a culture.

That piping hot *masala dosa** straight off the griddle slathered with butter and served with a spicy *sambar†* and a dollop of coconut chutney in India. *Kartoffelpuffer‡* with *apfelmus§* at the Christmas markets in Germany. *Mamitas¶* selling delicious and healthy *nabo*** served with *moto††* at the Cusco and Pisac market in Peru.

Street food is one of the wonders to experience in countries like India, Taiwan, Indonesia, Malaysia, Latin America, Morocco, to name just a few. The smells and sounds of the open-air food stalls and watching the cooks dish up colorful local delicacies right before your eyes is nothing short of a mouthwatering experience.

Even countries that don't have a street food culture but hold an appreciation for that vibe have created spaces that mimic street food culture. A new "truck food" or "food van" culture offers budget-friendly food without compromising quality and taste in the USA. Reffen in Copenhagen is an "urban playground for co-creation, innovation, food and creativity—and last but not least—the largest street food market in the Nordics."

Why would you not try it? The only reason I can think is hygiene concerns.

How clean is the place? Are the cooks following hygiene stan-dards? Are the drinks made from drinking water? In the USA or the EU, the regulations around food quality and hygiene are strictly enforced. In other places, I suggest taking these precautions.

- Eat at busy places. The food will be fresh.
- Lean towards eating only cooked food, preferably hot, and

---

*   *masala dosa*, thin crepe made from fermented rice and lentils and filled with spiced potatoes
†   *sambar*, spicy dense soup made with lentils, vegetables, and spices
‡   *Kartoffelpuffer*, German potato pancakes
§   *apfelmus*, German apple sauce cooked with cinnamon
¶   *mamitas*, local affectionate way to address the native Andean women
**   *nabo*, nutritious green leafy vegetable similar to mustard greens native to the Peruvian Andes cooked with potatoes
††   *moto*, boiled grains of Peruvian corn

avoid raw food like salads.

- Don't buy cut fruit from street stands. Prefer to buy the whole fruit and cut it yourself.

- If the food is exposed and there are many flies around, avoid eating there.

- Don't drink water in these places unless you can be sure that the water is clean.

- Ask for drinks without ice when unsure whether drinking water was used to make the ice.

Read Reviews

Read the restaurants' reviews on websites like **TripAdvisor** and **Yelp**, but take these with a pinch of salt. Because truth be told, there are ways to skew these reviews in this age of digital marketing. Friends and family are recruited to post five-star reviews. Competitors post 1-star reviews. Also, consider that just because fifteen people like that Thai restaurant you are thinking of going to does not mean you will like it. Everyone is different.

Use the reviews as another source of information, but finally, use your judgment and take the chance.

Medical Care

Pharmacies, clinics & hospital

One of the first things to do in a new country is to locate a pharmacy, clinic, and hospital closest to your rental. Is there a 24-hour pharmacy nearby? Pharmacies and local clinics are the primary go-to for common ailments like flu, cough, fever, and diarrhea. In most countries, a visit to the local clinic is relatively simple. You walk in, sign at the reception, and wait for a doctor to see you.

If you need a hospital for more serious concerns, find out:

- Does the hospital have English-speaking doctors?
- Will they accept your travel health insurance?

Save all the bills and receipts so you can get them reimbursed from your travel health insurance provider.

Alternative medical care

In many countries, alternative health care options that take a holistic approach to illnesses and provide natural remedies are available. For instance, Ayurveda, an ancient mind, body, and soul healing modality that originated in India, is now available in many countries. Homeopathy is equally well-known, and it might be relatively easy to locate a Homeopathy practitioner where you are. Local herbs to heal common ailments have been a part of many traditions. These practices are still alive in many regions. Check your local contacts to find herbalists nearby. Chinese medicine is another well-known alternative healing modality.

In all likelihood, your travel health insurance will not cover these. But these alternative medical practitioners are quite affordable. Take advantage of these modalities.

How to find medical help

Apart from asking your landlord or posting a query on the local expat Facebook group, **IAMAT** (International Association for Medical Assistance to Travelers) is an excellent resource to locate English-speaking health care providers in the member countries.

The Conscious Slow Traveler

#1 Say NO to plastic.

Nowadays, more and more people are aware of the importance of reducing plastic usage. You won't stick out like a sore thumb anymore for adhering to your green lifestyle. It might even be appreciated more than you realize.

- If you have to buy water, buy the largest sized bottles and fill your non-plastic bottle as and when you need it. Avoid buying small plastic water bottles.
- Take your Tupperware with you for takeout.
- Instead of buying pre-packaged food, buy fresh, unpackaged food whenever possible.

- Take a few cloth/linen bags with you when you go shopping. Always keep one in your daypack. That way, you will be covered for those spontaneous buys while you are out and about.

- No matter how much I try, I still end up with plastic bags. Collect and reuse them. Or give them away to a local organization that converts them into something useful. I know a nonprofit in Kerala, India, where a women's co-operative knits old plastic bags into stunningly colorful eco-shopping bags. Jump online and seek similar organizations near you.

- In a café, insist on getting your drink in a regular cup or a glass instead of in a plastic container. Isn't it more delightful to drink from a real cup or a glass? Take your mug or bottle with you when you want a drink to-go.

- Keep a bamboo/steel straw or a straw bottle such as **LifeStraw** in your daypack and ask for "No straw, please" at restaurants, cafes, etc. Cut the plastic straws.

#2 Say NO to having an endangered species on your meal plate.

Here is a known list of endangered species when writing this book:

bluefin tuna, sturgeon (caviar), whale meat, shark, tiger, pangolin, sea turtle meat and eggs, puffins, civet coffee.

The **World Wildlife Fund** keeps track of endangered species and their extinction status. If you feel concerned, check there for the most updated information.

#3 Go local.

Shop for your food needs with local shops instead of big-chain stores and supermarkets. Put more of your dollars into the pockets of the neighborhood small mom-n-pop stores, local markets, and local family run restaurants.

Resources

	App	Website	Cost
Online ordering	Amazon Shopping Mercado Libre Flipkart	amazon.com mercadolibre.com (for Latin America) flipkart.com (for India)	Free
Finding restaurants/cafes for specific dietary needs	Vegan Food Near You – HappyCow Tripadvisor	happycow.net yelp.com tripadvisor.com	Free
Finding medical resources in a foreign country		iamat.org	Free
Endangered species list	WWF Together	worldwildlife.org	Free

CHAPTER 18

MONEY-WISE ON THE ROAD

NOVEMBER 2019 - GUANAJUATO, MEXICO

"I need to get cash out." I pointed to the Santander ATM as we passed the Teatro Juarez on De Sopeña.

Mia, the New Yorker, had kindly offered to show me around the charming little town of Guanajuato. It was my second day there. As we walked around the city, replete with bright yellow marigold flowers, colorful masks, street fairs, fireworks, and painted skulls for the famous Mexican Day of the Dead celebration, I realized I needed to withdraw money.

"Don't use Santander or HSBC. Let's walk to Citibanamex," Mia suggested.

"Why not? Their transaction fee is reasonable," I was curious to know.

"I don't like Santander and HSBC. You see, they play this ATM exchange rate trick."

"What trick?" I was perplexed. By then, I had been in Mexico for six months but had not heard about it.

"Oh, you don't know?"

"I don't think so. What is it?" I queried.

"Well, what they try to do is earn a little extra commission above the transaction fee by offering you an exchange rate lower than your bank. Let's say that your home bank provides an exchange rate of 19.5. The Santander and HSBC ATMs offer you a slightly reduced exchange rate by prompting you this question during your withdrawal process:

'Our exchange rate is 18.5. Do you accept?'

At this point, if you choose 'Yes,' it will dispense the cash at the rate of 18.5 instead of 19.5, and they earned an extra *peso* per dollar. But if you choose 'No,' the ATM goes in a 'wait mode.' You might think that it is canceling your transaction because you said No. But don't walk away! Wait. Because after about thirty seconds, the ATM will dispense the cash at the rate of 19.5!"

"What? So, the local bank just tried to make an extra *peso* per dollar on top of charging the transaction fee?"

"Yeah! That's right. Thugs, aren't they?" she joked.

"That's ridiculous! How did you find out about this?" I was stunned at this new piece of information.

"I have lived here for six years. I should know a few local tricks by now!" She chuckled.

"I am sure there are other banks as well. I just know that Citibanamex doesn't play this game. It's not a lot of money, come to think of it. But it adds up. I rather use that money for one more nice meal at a local restaurant or buy another delicious home-made apple pie from lovely Anna than give it to a bank," she added.

I concurred with her.

Local tricks can only be learned from locals or other travelers on the ground.

* * *

Payment/Money Transfer Services to Use on the Road

In 2018, my ATM card was "swallowed" by an ATM in Cusco after dispensing me the money. The process of getting the card back from the bank was going to take a few weeks. In the meantime, I needed more cash for my impending trip to Huaraz in the North of Peru. Elise, my photographer friend graciously offered to withdraw some money from her bank account to help me out. As she handed me the money, in the same instant, I logged into my PayPal account on my iPhone and paid her back. Within a couple of minutes, our transaction was over.

PayPal payment service is one of the most useful payment services I have used while on the road. There are situations where cash or a credit card will not be helpful, but PayPal will be. Such as when I had to pay back Elise. Another instance of using PayPal is paying for workshops where they may not have a credit card payment set up, and the amount is too large to pay by cash.

It is easy, safe, and instantaneous. Once you link your bank account to your PayPal account, all you need is your name or email to pay or get paid as long as the receiver or the sender is set up with PayPal. **Zelle** and **Venmo** are equally popular though I haven't felt the need to use them.

They work with most of the currencies in the world. For payments into foreign accounts, there is a small fee involved. But the convenience of making a payment while on the road offsets the cost, to be honest.

Xoom is an equally reliable and secure money transfer service. You can send money to a bank account, send cash to be picked up at partner locations, or have it delivered to your recipient's door. There is a limit on how much money you can send, and the transaction fee varies based on several factors. It is best to investigate the details on Xoom's website. The transfer takes two to three business days.

Wise is another reliable and secure money transfer service, used more often to transfer large amounts of money from one bank account to another. While on the slow road, if you find that perfect house on the beach and decide to buy it, you can use Wise to transfer large amounts of money from your home bank account to the seller's bank account. Their transaction fee is higher than Xoom but less than a regular wire transfer from the bank. They do offer a better exchange rate than Xoom, your bank, or other money transfer services. The transfer takes two to three business days.

A new trend in making payments without using a card is using **Apple Pay** or **Google Pay**. Instead of inserting a card into a machine, you hold your phone near a contactless reader. The reader recognizes your fingerprint or your face and authorizes the payment. The London Underground has made it convenient for riders to buy tickets using this system. Several countries have not ramped up to this form of payment yet. Set it up on your phone anyway in case you can use it. It is a more secure way to make payments than using a credit card.

5 Tips for Getting Cash on the Road with Zero or Less Fees

#1 Identify foreign country ATMs that partner with your bank.

Using ATMs in the partner network allows you to withdraw cash without any transaction fees. Call your bank and ask them which banks they partner with in the country you are going to.

#2 Don't use credit cards to withdraw cash at ATMs.

These are considered cash advances, you will likely not get a reasonable exchange rate, and you will be charged an interest rate for payments, just like using a credit card. According to **Credit-Cards'** 2017 cash advance survey, the average cash advance APR is 23.68%, with a typical fee of 5 percent of the advance or $10, whichever is greater. Keep this option only for emergencies.

#3 Ask your bank if they will refund the transaction fees.

Explain to them that you will be on an extended journey. Sometimes the bank will do so depending on your status and account type.

#4 Withdraw the maximum possible amount from the ATM.

After living in a place for a few weeks, you will locate ATMs that allow you to withdraw a higher amount in one withdrawal. It will reduce the number of trips you make, reduce the risk of fraud, and reduce the transaction fee due to fewer withdrawals.

#5 Locate ATMs that charge the lowest transaction fees and offer the highest withdrawal at a time.

"Nova Scotia charged me 70 *pesos* for cash withdrawal, and I could get only 7,000 *pesos* at a time!" Matt sat down next to me on a bench outside the Santo Domingo church, clearly exasperated with his banking experience. Do you remember Matt from San Miguel de Allende? The one who could not travel without his portable speakers? We had crossed paths again in Oaxaca city.

I had just finished my usual Saturday afternoon sketching session at the IAGO (Instituto de Artes Graficas de Oaxaca).

"What? That's ridiculous. I use Banco Populare. They charge me 19 *pesos* per transaction, and I can withdraw 15,000 *pesos* in one go," I offered my tip while sipping *tejate*[*] and eyeing the fresh potato chips at the street stand to our right.

"No, no, no. I know what you are thinking. No more chips for you!" Matt admonished with sincerity. He had taken the responsibility of breaking my addiction to these potato chips found at corner stands all over Oaxaca center.

"Now I know where to get my cash from," Matt said as we sauntered down the pedestrian road towards the Museo Textil de Oaxaca on Miguel Hidalgo. We had planned to see an exhibition of Zapotec rugs weaved using the Indigo and Cochineal pigments.

Do you catch my drift?

9 Tips for Staying Money-wise on the Road

#1 Always pay in local currency at the point of sale and in cash.

You might see signs like "Pay in USD or Euros" in kiosks, small stores, travel agencies, bus companies, restaurants, hotels, etc.

Never pay in USD or Euros in a foreign country at a point-of-sale. Pay in cash in the local currency. While it is tempting and may feel safer and convenient from an accounting perspective to pay using USD or Euros, it will not be to your advantage. Most likely, you will get a low exchange rate.

#2 Plan your cash withdrawals wisely when changing countries.

Don't withdraw too much cash in the current local currency right before you plan to travel to a different country. Otherwise, you will be left with a lot of money from "here" when you cross the border. If you try to convert that money back to USD or Euros, you will only lose in the exchange.

---

[*]   *tejate,* a mildly sweet frothy cacao and corn drink typical to Oaxaca

#3 Try to spend all the coins and small notes regularly.

Don't wait for the last minute. When you cross borders, coins and small notes become useless. I keep a few with me on purpose as part of my growing collection of coins and bills from different countries.

#4 Keep 50 to 100 USD/Euro in cash somewhere safe.

They can be useful in unknown situations or emergencies. Consider this. You are crossing an international border by road, you have to pay an exit tax that you did not know about, they only accept USD/Euro, and there is no ATM at the border crossing. Or the banks go on strike, and all the ATMs stop working because there is no one to fill them.

#5 Always use a bank ATM to get cash.

Avoid "independent" ATMs, such as Travelex, Euronet, Moneybox, etc. These have high fees. They are often located next to bank ATMs, hoping travelers will be too confused to notice the difference. Don't believe any marketing signs such as "Get cash for free" that you might see.

Always use a bank ATM, preferably an ATM at the bank location itself. The chances of these machines being ATM card skimmers is less.

#6 Withdraw cash from an ATM in a safe location and during standard day times.

As soon as you have entered your PIN or once you have cash in hand, you are most vulnerable to theft. Always plan to withdraw during the day time.

#7 Use money exchange services only if the difference between the buy and sell rates is less than 10%.

That is a reasonably fair transaction.

#8 Become comfortable with the local currency.

It helps to keep the expenses in check. Suppose I am in Indonesia and my monthly budget is $1000. According to the conversion rate in Indonesia, that is approximately 14 million IDR when writing this book. When looking for a house to rent, if I get a 7 million IDR quote per month, which would be 50% of my monthly budget, I know it's expensive.

If the local market vendor sells spinach for 10,000 IDR, it takes a little practice to get around all the zeroes and work out the math that 10,000 IDR means $0.75. That is cheap! As you can see, it is about getting comfortable with the exchange rate, the denominations, and the number of zeroes in some instances.

Most of us are not used to paying in millions!

#9 Get your VAT refund in Europe before you leave.

In Europe, all sales have a VAT (Value Added Tax) automatically added to the sale price. The VAT can range from 8% to 27%, depending on the goods. The good news is that VAT on some things such as coats, jackets, bags, etc., is refundable. But it is not for things like groceries, eating in restaurants, or for your accommodation.

To dig deeper into VAT refunds in the EU, do an internet search for *"VAT refunds for EU visitors"* and don't forget to get yours before you leave.

Resources

	App	Website	Cost
Payment/ Transfer services	PayPal Venmo Zelle Xoom Money Wise Apple Wallet Google Pay	paypal.com venmo.com zellepay.com xoom.com wise.com apple.com/apple-pay (Apple Pay) wallet.google.com (Google Pay)	Commission for services may be charged.

Chapter 19

Cybersecurity

October 2012 - Copenhagen, Denmark

The last place I expected to be a victim of fraud was in Finland.

I landed at the Helsinki airport on a quick day trip from Copenhagen for an interview with a potential client. Since the currency in Finland is Euros, and I only had Danish *Kroners* (I was living in Copenhagen at that time), I needed to withdraw cash in Euros. I did so using my US ATM card from an ATM at the airport.

My future client manager took me to an Indian restaurant for lunch and an interview-cum-chat. I landed the consulting assignment and returned to Copenhagen the same night, happy with the outcome.

A few days later, Chrissy, my roommate, and I were enjoying some *hygge** time over wine in our cozy living room. The weather in Copenhagen was turning from long summer days into short, cold, and dark winter days. For a peculiar reason, my gut told me I should check my bank account. So, I logged in, as I do from time to time. What I saw shocked me! Withdrawal transactions at little kiosks all over St. Petersburg, Russia totaling approximately $650!

I blinked my eyes thinking I was seeing wrong. When did I go to St. Petersburg?

"Chrissy," I yelled out to my roommate, who was in the kitchen preparing a platter of cheese to go with the wine, "do you remember me telling you I was going to St. Petersburg?"

"St. Petersburg? I thought you went to Helsinki, didn't you?"

I thought so too.

---

* *hygge*, a Danish concept implying quiet comfort, coziness, and focusing on simple pleasures of life

"Then why do I see these transactions on my card in St. Petersburg?" I sought an explanation.

Chrissy ran over to my desk and peered at my laptop's screen over my shoulder.

"Did you lose your card?" she asked, raising her eyebrows in a-la-Chrissy as if admonishing a child.

I hadn't. It was still safely snuggled in my wallet.

We looked at each other for a moment before exclaiming in a chorus,

"Fraud!"

Alarmed, I took a deep breath and called my bank. They verified that the transactions had indeed happened in St. Petersburg, ascertaining fraudulent activity. At my request, they immediately canceled the card, initiated a fraud case, and returned the amount to my account within a week.

It turned out that the ATM I had used at the Helsinki airport had a card skimmer that captured my PIN and the details encoded on my ATM card's magnetic strip. Later, I learned that cards with magnetic strips are more susceptible to fraud than cards with an EMV chip. The new card I received from my bank was with an EMV chip. Thank goodness!

I learned that it doesn't matter where you are. Cyber theft can happen anywhere.

* * *

In this digital age, crime and theft are no longer only personal and physical. We check the internet quite often. We store much of our personal information online and on our phones and laptops. We access our accounts online. According to CNBC's article on seven tips for staying safe while traveling:

> In 2016, more than 15 million Americans were victims of identity theft, up 16 percent from the previous year, according to Experian, a global information services group. About 33 percent of that fraud took place when people were traveling.

These numbers are for Americans alone. There is also the rest of the world to consider.

Cybersecurity is a rabbit-hole. An extensive number of articles have been written about the topic, all of which highlight that these days with our increasing reliance on digital technology, cybersecurity and protecting one's personal data is more critical than ever before. In this chapter, I will not delve into the depths of cybersecurity but share simple everyday tips you can use while on and off the road.

13 Tips for Cybersecurity

#1 Always use legitimate Wi-Fi spots when outside.

Avoid connecting to networks that are not password protected. If you must do so, don't log into social media, banks, etc.

#2 If your devices are not password-protected, do it now.

We store valuable information on our phones and other devices such as passwords, banking information, personal photos, etc. The last thing we want is for this data to end up in the wrong hands. So, set up a strong password on all your digital devices.

#3 Log out completely on public computers.

If you have accessed any of your accounts from an internet cafe or other public computers such as a library, remember to log out completely. When you log in, uncheck the option "Remember me" or "Stay logged in" which are checked by default.

If you don't explicitly uncheck them, your login ID will be "remembered" on that computer even after you have logged out. It will display to the next person who uses the same machine.

#4 Clear the browser's cache, history, and cookies.

Some public computers could be loaded with malware like key-word logging programs that track everything you type, including passwords. If you must log in to sensitive accounts from public computers, remember to leave no trace.

How do you do that?

The way to clear a browser's cache, history, and cookies is different for different browsers, so I won't try to generalize the instructions here. A quick internet search for *"how to clear browser cache, history and cookies for <browser name>"* will pop-up several how-to articles.

Delete these from your laptop as well regularly.

#5 Set up a 2-step verification on all your sensitive accounts.

2-step verification requires you to enter not only your password but also a code sent over email, text message, or an **Authenticator** app. Not all online accounts offer this option. But if they do, then set it up. It provides an extra layer of security against cyber theft.

#6 Monitor your financial accounts regularly to ensure there has been no fraud.

If you have used your card over an unsecured Wi-Fi network or a public computer, watch your financial accounts for a few days to ensure no theft. Regardless, it's better to set up reminders to check your sensitive accounts from time to time.

Word of caution:

Never access your financial accounts from a computer other than yours.

#7 Never share sensitive information such as your credit card details, password, internet banking IDs, etc., over the phone, email, SMS, messaging apps, or other social media accounts.

That's it. Nothing more to say here.

#8 Consider using a secure browser.

Unlike regular browsers, secure browsers protect us from personal information leaks due to browser fingerprinting, tracking cookies, and other malware, adware, and spyware that are floating on the World Wide Web in search of victims. My favorite browser is **Brave**. Other secure browsers are **Opera, Google Chrome,** and **Vivaldi**. Doing an internet search for the *"most secure browsers 2020"* will give you the complete list with all the pros and cons.

#9 Use safe search engines that don't track and record your browsing activity.

My favorite search engines are **Duckduckgo** and **Ecosia.** Or do an internet search for *"Best private search engines"* and you will get a list with all the pros and cons.

#10 Augment your device security by using a VPN service.

VPN services like **Proton, NordVPN, ExpressVPN,** and **Tunnel-Bear** provide another security layer when used with a secure browser. A VPN is especially useful when traveling to countries like China, where you cannot access social networking sites like Facebook, Instagram, Twitter, YouTube, Pinterest, and all Google services. But you can access them over VPN.

#11 Install a "Find my phone/device" type of app and a wiping software on your devices.

In 2018, my iPhone was stolen from my handbag while I was traveling in a crowded bus from Pisac to Huasau in the Sacred Valley of the Incas, Peru. Huasau, a quiet hamlet an hour's ride away from Cusco, is recognized amongst the local Andeans as the place to visit traditional healers. I was visiting Wilca, an experienced healer in the community and a dear soul sister.

I walked into her healing room filled with various sacred objects she used in her practice—*Koka* leaves, condor feathers, flowers, incense, candles and other sacred objects juxtaposed with pictures from the Christian faith. She immediately called my phone to see if the pickpocket would pick up. But alas, no one answered.

I decided to use the "Find my phone" app from my Mac to track my phone. It showed the location to be Cusco. Through this app, I was able to send a message that the thief could see flashing on the phone screen.

"I will pay you 200 *soles* if you return my phone."

He replied back in agreement!

We met in Cusco an hour later on a seedy, packed street and did the spooky exchange. He would have earned less than two hundred *soles* in the stolen goods market for my iPhone. Instead, he got a better deal within a couple of hours.

If your device is stolen or lost, it's not only a loss of a device which can be replaced. The more significant loss is all the personal information like photos, messages, etc., that could get into the wrong hands. Install a "Find my Device" type of app on all your devices and link them together. This type of app shows you exactly where your lost or stolen device (e.g., phone) is on a map from another (e.g., laptop) if they are linked together. And you might just be able to retrieve it as I was.

If it cannot be recovered, then to be safe, it is best to wipe out everything from it remotely. You can do this with the help of a wiping software that usually comes along with the 'Find my Device' type of app.

#12 Pay more ahead of time to reduce the number of online transactions.

I keep my US phone number with T-Mobile, but with the bare minimum plan. Instead of logging in every month to make the payment, I pay for six months in advance. The T-Mobile system automatically deducts the monthly charge from the advance payment, saving me from remembering to log in and pay for my phone bill every month. This way, I reduce the number of times I have to do a financial transaction while on the road.

#13 Backup frequently and regularly.

I prefer to carry an external hard drive with me to backup all of my device data. But backing up on the cloud is more convenient. With your data being on the cloud, it is easy to access from anywhere and anytime without the need for carrying a clunky external hard drive. **BackBlaze** provides decent plans for cloud backups.

Okay. I will get off this soapbox now. ═)

The Conscious Slow Traveler

#1 Make a green choice.

When choosing which search engine to use, I prefer to use Ecosia. Every time I search using Ecosia, the company donates to a tree-planting project around the world. What I love about Ecosia is its full transparency into the tree-planting projects they support. An added advantage is that if I feel passionate about devoting my time towards the cause of tree-planting, I have a curated and genuine list of worldwide organizations available. All I need to do is contact the organization I am interested in to find out about volunteer or other opportunities.

Resources

	App	Website	Cost
Safe browsers	Brave Google Chrome Opera Touch web browser Vivaldi (only for Android phones)	brave.com google.com/ chrome opera.com vivaldi.com	Free
Safe search engines	DuckDuckGo Ecosia	duckduckgo.com ecosia.org	Free
VPN services	ProtonVPN ExpressVPN NordVPN TunnelBear	protonvpn.com expressVPN.com nordvpn.com tunnelbear.com	Monthly/Yearly subscription.
2-Step account authentication	Authenticator		Free
Backups	Backblaze	backblaze.com	Free basic version. Subscription-based for more features.

Section IV

In A Relationship

*Travel spins us round in two ways at once:
It shows us the sights and values and issues
that we might ordinarily ignore; but it also,
and more deeply, shows us all the parts of
ourselves that might otherwise grow rusty.*

Pico Iyer

Chapter 20

The Challenges

It is perhaps 6 a.m. or 7 a.m. You have landed after a fifteen-hour flight. You make your way to your short-term accommodation in a shared van. The town is still waking up from the night's slumber. The narrow streets are empty except for the school kids in a blue and white uniform running to school. Occasionally you see a lone someone sweeping the sidewalks or a taxi passing by. The early morning mist is rolling in from the surrounding mountains.

You drop off your luggage and walk the eight blocks to *El Zócalo*[*]. There is a lazy candor at the local market surrounding it. Vendors are unpacking their stalls, a few grabbing a quick breakfast of piping hot *tamales*[†], *champurrado*[‡], and *café de olla*[§] from the street vendors on bicycles. The morning air is crisp and fresh. You settle down with a hot *café de olla* in a mud cup on a bench in the park and breathe in the scene. A feeling of excitement begins to bubble up inside you—that of unlocking the mysteries of a new place and, through it, discovering a hidden piece of you. A thought arrives riding on the aroma of the freshly brewed coffee, teasing your senses.

I could live here!

The enchantment of a new place *is* due to its freshness and newness. To wake up in a strange town, not knowing anyone, not knowing anything, is an irresistible invitation to untangle and demystify. Those first few weeks are like the initial stages of a budding new romance filled with limitless curiosity, playful discoveries, and moments of sweet rapture.

---

[*]   *El Zócalo*, a term used to refer to the main square of many Mexican towns
[†]   *tamales*, fluffy and steamed corn dough pockets filled with meat, beans, and cheese or vegetables
[‡]   *champurrado*, a thick, hearty, maize-based drink with chocolate
[§]   *café de olla*, a traditional Mexican coffee brewed with spices such as cinnamon, cloves, and star anise

How do the sunrises and sunsets look from this corner of the earth? Is the moon here just as big as it was in higher altitudes? How does the rhythm of the local language sound?

What is the local beer called? What are the local delicacies? Which festivals are coming up? What are a couple of commonly used swear words? Are there any local fruits or vegetables that you have never tasted before? How are women treated in this society?

 Capture this newness with your inner lens and hold onto it as long as you can!

Because once the first rush of a new romance begins to settle, the challenges of being in a relationship will start to creep in. Didn't I say right at the beginning that like anything else in life that's worth doing, slow traveling will come with its challenges?

* * *

The Downsides

Don't be fooled by the constant stream of lively photos posted on Facebook and Instagram by travelers. Being away from home, friends, and family, intertwined with the challenges of a new culture, a foreign language, and different food, can cause stress and anxiety.

We face loneliness.

We miss people and activities from the life we used to know.

We start to recognize what we took for granted.

Over time, we feel the distance between who we used to be in a world we used to know and who we are now in the new world we find ourselves in. We leave fragments of ourselves behind and uncover new pieces along this slow road traversed.

How can the familiar "old me" integrate with the sometimes contradictory "new me"?

Being on the slow travel trails has its upsides, but it can also be tough. Here are some of the most common challenges that we encounter while on the slow travel road.

New place, new people fatigue

There comes a time when we *don't* want to meet new people. We *don't* want to go to a new place and start all over again. All we long for is to disappear into the lap of comfort and familiarity.

Take a break from the local culture and people.

What gives you a feeling of comfort and familiarity?

Mac-n-cheese? A pot of warm soup? Reading magazines and news from back home? Disappear into the lobby of a five-star hotel where a big brushstroke of intercontinental business has swept over all hints of the local culture. Slip into a different world by going to the movies or sitting down with your favorite novel. I like to make a tub of popcorn or *mung daal khichdi* or a chai and settle down with a good old Bollywood movie on my laptop.

It can do wonders for the struggling traveler's spirit.

Reconnect with your Why, the purpose for this travel and examine—are you done?

Marijntje, "the little mother of the river Rhine" who has now made her home in Chinchero in the Sacred Valley of the Incas, thinks that *"if you feel traveler's fatigue, then you are not traveling slowly enough!"*

It makes sense. Don't be afraid of putting down roots in your present home. Slow down even more and stay for longer.

Loneliness

Let's face it.

Loneliness is something that uncannily hits us all, looping us into a myriad of existential questions. Does it have anything to do with traveling?

I posit that it is a myth that loneliness solely strikes those on the road. We can feel the heavy and sharp pain of loneliness, even in our daily work, home, and friends and family routine. It can hit the best of us even when everything in life is seemingly sorted and lined up into place. For some, loneliness at home *is* the very reason to venture onto the travel trails. It is a way for them to bring back the lost spark and to redefine themselves.

But loneliness hits us a tad bit harder when on travel trails where we are outside our comfort zone. We don't have immediate access to call upon friends or family for a good cuppa.

I see it as a time to peer deep within myself and listen to my soul's yearnings and angst. What is it whispering ever so softly? I take refuge in my paintbrush and let it transport my feelings and thoughts onto paper. When it becomes unbearable, loneliness compels me to reach out to people whereas otherwise, being an introvert, I would have hesitated to do so.

 The slow travel track has not made me more alone. It has pushed me to become a more connected human being who is comfortable with solitude.

Here are some loneliness busters.

Put yourself out there.

One of the fantabulous things about being on the road is that other travelers are receptive to conversations. The underlying ethos being: "We are all sailing in the same boat."

The more we reach out to others, the more natural it becomes for us, often leading to the opposite of loneliness—friendships that span across time and continents. Take a leap of faith and put your vulnerable self out there.

Go for a walk in nature.

Nature is a miraculous antidote to combat loneliness. It teaches us the interconnection of life and that giving and receiving is the fundamental premise of building meaningful relationships; the lack of this understanding is often the root cause of loneliness.

Exercise, exercise, exercise.

Vigorous exercise like running laps, swimming, dancing, going to the gym, etc., will get your blood pumping as well as release a flood of feel-good endorphins in your system.

Engage in a creative activity.

Creativity is the primal energy of the universe and our existence. If you find yourself alone and feeling blue, what better way to commune with our reality than by unleashing your creative energy into a mindful project or activity?

Let your hair down.

Dare yourself to do something crazy that you have been postponing. Skydiving is on the top of my list. What's on yours? Going wild can be a cure! It can do wonders to shake away those rainy days, and in turn, it will leave you beaming and full of life.

Do something kind.

It is a well-known fact that random acts of kindness raise dopamine levels and is a mood booster. It doesn't have to be anything grand or impressive. Simple acts of selfless generosity such as offering to dog-sit when your neighbor wants to go out, picking up plastic on the beach, offering to teach English to your landlord's daughter, etc., can work like magic.

Find something in your immediate vicinity that is small, simple, and actionable.

Jane, the sparkly seventy-three-year-old British woman, goes out for walks and finds something in a stranger walking by that she genuinely likes.

"That's a beautiful scarf you are wearing," she'll say, or, "You have such lovely hair."

Can you imagine a lovely stranger stops in front of you and pays you a compliment? I would be taken back, but it would undoubtedly bring a smile to my face and lift me. For a moment, there is a connection, perhaps a few words exchanged. That makes Jane feel part of humanity all over again.

"That's all I need," she explained when asked how she handles loneliness while slow traveling.

Make a kindness calendar where you commit to doing a simple act of kindness each day or every so often. Here are a few ideas to get you going.

- Like Jane, give kind comments to as many people as you can, regardless of whether they are strangers you run into while on a walk or folks you know.
- Donate a little something to the local food bank or a charity in your neighborhood.
- Congratulate someone for their achievement, no matter how small.
- Reach out and chat with a friend or family who might be lonely or have not been well.
- Notice when you're being hard on yourself and be kind instead.
- Practice gratitude. List at least three things, people, or situations you are grateful for, even if they were challenging but helped you grow.
- Call someone who is far away to say hello and have a chat.

I miss ...

You!

There is no substitute for missing people we love and share a bond with. There isn't. We can, however, stay connected using social media even when far away. More on this in Chapter 22: Stay Connected! On the other hand, being away from people you know will quickly influence you to try and find new social connections in your new environment. After all, we are hardwired to being social.

Missing things is a little easier to handle. Such as that Heinz tomato ketchup that is a must with French fries. Or Marmite on buttered toast for breakfast. The truth is that there will not be a solution for everything you miss on the road, but you'll learn how to make the most of what is available.

Michael misses Starbucks coffee. But despite his whining about how *no one* can make better coffee than Starbucks does, which I'm afraid I have to disagree with, he thoroughly enjoys the coffee in his local neighborhood coffee shop in Calca, Peru.

Invariably, we learn that we can live quite well without many things that we would have otherwise thought impossible. We recognize that we do not need as much as we thought we did. A light begins to shine on all the things we took for granted. This shift stays with us after we return home and begin to navigate life there. Take this as an adventure to form new habits by becoming more adaptable.

Emma, the Swedish cyclist, described what she missed while cycling through South America.

> *"As a cyclist, what I missed most is a warm shower, the protection of four walls in a house, and the comfort of an actual bed. It made me feel and acknowledge how much I appreciated these things that I took for granted on a normal basis."*

Ordering online or having someone send over a care package is always an option. Oh, how that longing for what we miss becomes sweet rapture when we do get it!

 Whether we miss someone or something, either way, it's a lesson in detachment.

Saying goodbyes & continuity

The most difficult challenge I continuously face while on the slow road is saying goodbye and making peace with not having continuity in relationships. I meet someone wonderful, we spend some amazing times together, and feel a real soul connection with each other.

Then they leave. Or I do.

We move on with our travel plans, and there is a goodbye involved. Sometimes I don't want to say goodbye. In my quest for permanence and depth, I have to satisfy myself with depth. Slow travel is a big lesson in the impermanence of life. The lived lessons of detachment and letting go even when the heart is filled with sadness are palpable truths of slow travel life. The more I experience this, the more I see all of us as dancing stars in a cosmic-walk, crossing paths with each other when we have soul contracts to fulfill and then dancing away along our trajectory.

Then there is social media to stay connected over time and space.

There is looking forward to making a plan to meet again in the future somewhere in this grand earth-walk.

The feeling of home

Once you have been on this journey for a while, you will never be fully at home again in any one place because part of your heart will be somewhere else. Right now, I am at a breathtakingly beautiful beach in Tulum, Mexico. But I can't help but close my eyes and fantasize about whether or not I will return to the Sacred Valley of the Incas, Peru. The meaningful encounters from there and the felt sense of the sacred mountains linger.

As I wander down that memory lane, this song by Paul Young is playing synchronously in the bar next door on the beach.

"Every time you go away, you take a piece of me with you."

Except that I change it to:

"Every time I go away, I leave a piece of me with you."

 That is the price we pay for the richness of loving and living in different places.

The question, where is home arises from time to time. Again, a song by Paul Young comes to my rescue.

"Wherever I lay my hat, that's my home."

Except that I change it to:

"Wherever I lay my heart, that's my home."

Over time, I have discovered that the feeling of home is internal and portable. It is not attached to my birth identity or the passport I carry. I can feel at home in many corners of this world because each land and its people have unfurled a different facet of me. Paradoxically, it is only through traveling and living in many places that I found myself—integrated and whole—and at home with myself. If I was a suitcase, then slow travel unpacked me and put me back together again.

Remember the "What can I NOT live without?" list that you

packed? Those are the things with which we create a sense of home away from home. I can visualize Tamara pulling out one of her pre-moistened individually packed facial masks to rest, refresh, and meditate. And Matt listening to music on his portable speakers to recharge his batteries.

Another way to create a home away from home is by developing relationships for everyday needs. By that, I mean going to the same bakery for buying bread, the same laundry for washing clothes, the same neighborhood store for daily needs, the same pharmacy for medicines, the same vegetable vendor for produce, and so on. The more we patron the same businesses, the more the sense of familiarity and hence the relationship grows. Establishing a routine provides a structure in the new life and environment around you.

 The more familiar we become and establish a routine, the higher the felt sense of home.

CHAPTER 21

DON'T LET ALL THAT GET YOU DOWN

Because as Paul Young has sung, "Nothing's gonna stop us now..."

I read somewhere that self-care rituals are the new sexy. I think they are. I boil it down to a three-pronged strategy: taking care of the body, mind, and soul.

Seriously, taking care of our bodies is something we do every day. But the other two, the mind and the soul, also need to be nurtured and nourished and all the more so while slow traveling.

Cultivate a Daily Practice & Routine

What out of your typical day at home can you port to your life on the road? Cultivating a daily practice helps to stay grounded and alleviates travel anxiety. A few examples are yoga, meditation, tai-chi, mindful breathing, movement exercises, martial arts, and running.

Here is how my daily practice and routine looks like:

I start my day early with an hour of daily meditation practice with yoga incorporated into it twice a week, followed by a nutritious breakfast, the most important meal of my day. I make it a point to walk every day for at least an hour by running errands, going shopping for little needs, exploring a new neighborhood on foot, or walking to social events.

Kriszta, the one who left her "shiny" management job, is a sports fanatic. Her daily schedule consists of sports, sports, and sports — two hours of surfing in the morning and one hour of weight training in the afternoon.

Keep a Journal

Capture the simple, ordinary, and everyday moments occurring in an extraordinary life on the slow road. Journaling helps to put our experiences into perspective and lets us reflect later on this unique snapshot of time from our life.

Who knows? The journal might end up becoming a best-seller!

Journaling has helped me make sense of myself and the world I am experiencing on my slow travel trails. It shows me where I have been, who I am, who I could be, and how I locate myself in the new place.

Vineeth, a fellow author says:

"I always keep a pen and anything to write on because, in slow travel, you are sure to be at your intellectual best, especially when you are stuck at the bus station waiting for the bus that never came!"

He probably wrote part of his book on a few such occasions.

Find Community

When we are on the road for a longer time, we are travelers but not. We long for some aspects of being at home—one of them being cultivating a semblance of a healthy social life. Beyond the logistics of finding an apartment, scouting ways for local transportation and such, there is a genuine need to find a community. After all, we, as human beings, are tribal creatures. Relationships are part of who we are as species. The people we meet become the most enriching, memorable, and life-changing part of travel.

During my time in Bali in 2018, I started going for biweekly life sketching sessions hosted by Pranoto, an amazing Balinese artist, at his studio and gallery. Not only did I forge a strong connection with him that continues to sustain till date, at his studio, I met other expats and local artists. Soon I found myself receiving invitations for social gatherings, art openings, and live music evenings.

At **Hubud**, a co-working space in Ubud, I met many digital nomads and expanded my knowledge of digital marketing. Through them, I discovered a bitcoin group that met weekly. Not only did I learn a lot about bitcoin, other cryptocurrencies, and cybersecurity, but I also met inspiring and innovative people who had made Bali their long-term home.

Ask yourself, what do you enjoy doing? What do you wish to learn? How do you want to spend your time on your slow travel?

Yoga, tai chi, meditation, surfing, quantum theory, writing groups, art, photography, dance, Bohm dialogues, volunteering with local communities, teaching English, courses to upgrade your skills, learning a new language, learning to make beer, learning to cook the local cuisine, hiking…

The choices are endless.

There are several ways to locate activities, events, classes, and gatherings in your area. Once you meet a few people, that will get the ball rolling. From there, you will meet others and find new activities and groups to connect with.

- Join groups on **Facebook** and **Meetups** that are related to your areas of interest. For instance, if you want to connect with other Digital Nomads, search for *"digital nomads"* on Facebook or Meetups.

- If there is no group or event related to what you desire to do, don't be shy and create one on Facebook or Meetups. You will be surprised how many people were simply waiting around for someone else to begin!

- **InterNations** is another networking group of working professionals. Join one if there is one in your area.

- Do an internet search for *"co-working spaces <city name>"* if you want a semiformal working environment, connect with remote workers, and learn new skills.

- Some travelers use **Tinder** as a way to meet people instead of for dating.

- Ask around for local volunteering opportunities through the people you meet.

- Search out cafes known for their "hangout" culture, and cultivate the habit of starting conversations with strangers. Put yourself out there.

One way I enjoy exchanging culture with other travelers, expats, and locals I meet is by inviting them to celebrate important festivals and events with me. They love being included. It opens the pandora's box for a rich discussion on the commonalities and differences between different cultures, the origins, and the beliefs underlying these customs.

While some of us have to find ways to meet people, Glen's dog does that for him!

> *"We are traveling with our dog, and it can be an amazing way to meet people and have conversations. Just today, a family started talking to us about our dog, but it quickly turned into an invitation to their house and sharing a beer while talking about the world."*

Share Your Travels

It is enriching to form new connections and friends from different parts of the world. Yet, a part of us longs to stay connected with people who knew the "old" us and take them along this journey where we are changing, somewhere deep down in our bones. In short, we miss people we have known and built bonds with who are not near us.

Share your travel adventures and stories with them. Don't leave them out on the extraordinary life you are living and let them live it vicariously through you.

- Set up reminders on your calendar to give you a little beep on birthdays and anniversaries of people who matter. I like to send a photo I have taken along my travels, edit it with a personal wish, and a note about where I took that photo. It adds a personal touch and loops them into my travel trails.

- Share photos and news of your travels through social media platforms like Facebook, Instagram, and SmugMug. Start a blog.

- Send out "Visit Me!" invitations to friends and family. If you have kept them updated with your travel tales, that will surely tempt them to visit.

Indulge Yourself

YES! A big part of my self-care ritual is to indulge myself with a wellness treatment like massage or spa therapy from time to time. It does wonders for my health to pamper myself with some luxury.

Every once in a while, splurging on a fancy accommodation can go a long way. Don't miss out on indulgent moments, especially if they're unique to the location you've settled in for the time being, such as the *hammam** baths in Turkey or the *temezcals*[†] in Mexico, Guatemala, and Peru. Sweat it out and release all those feelings of anxiety, loneliness, uncertainty and such. An *Ayurvedic massage*[‡] or a *Panchakarma*[§] treatment in India will do wonders to balance your mind, body, and soul. Find natural hot springs in the region where you can soak in the healing mineral-rich waters. One of my favorite natural hot springs is tucked away at the base of *Apu Ausangate*[¶] in Peru at an altitude of approximately 6000m.

How do you love to pamper yourself? What's available in your Where?

---

* *hammam*, a Middle Eastern steam room intended as a ritual for cleansing the body
† *temezcals*, a traditional Mexican sweat lodge
‡ *Ayurvedic massage*, a treatment that incorporates the 5,000-year-old Indian principles of the science of life and pressure points
§ *Panchakarma*, a cleansing and rejuvenating treatment for the body, mind, and consciousness
¶ *Apu Ausangate*, spirit of the sacred mountain Ausangate, the fourth highest peak in the Andes of Peru

Chapter 22

Stay Connected!

There are many ways to stay connected with our loved ones, no matter where we are. The good news is that they are either *free* or *cheap*! Gone are the days when a single international telephone call could cause a gasp-inducing dent in our monthly budget.

Mobile Phones — Again

Get a local SIM card

Once your phone is unlocked, remove your home country SIM card (e.g., USA), plug in the local SIM card (e.g., Denmark), and start using your phone in the new country. A local SIM card comes in very handy when you need to make local calls to inquire about accommodation or in case you have to call the police, emergency services, or an ambulance.

The drawback is that you can no longer receive phone calls/messages on your home country number. So, if your boss thinks you are working remotely in the USA, tries to reach you on your US number but can't because you are on a beach in Australia with an Australian SIM card, then you will be in trouble. This problem can be resolved easily, as you will find out further on in this chapter.

If you get a local SIM card, remember to keep your home country SIM card safe. You can likely re-use it when you return—unless there is an expiration date for cards when not in use.

 My recommendation?

Get a local SIM card, whether with your home phone or a locally bought cheap phone.

Buy a local phone or use your home phone?

The other option is to keep your home country service alive while abroad with your home country number but buy a cheap local phone with a local SIM card for local calling/text purposes. This way, your home country phone will still be active and available for people to call/text you (and your boss won't know that you are in Australia if (s)he can get a hold of you on your number). But remember that you will pay for roaming, which will make it expensive. If you are running a business and not expecting too many calls, this may be the right solution.

Turn roaming off!

If you are using your home phone while abroad with your home country SIM card but do not expect/want phone calls or texts from your home country, remember to turn roaming *off!* Otherwise, you might unknowingly get hit with a high bill that you were not expecting. Inform people at home that you will be traveling and let them know to contact you only over messaging apps like WhatsApp or Signal.

The prepaid vs. postpaid SIM card debate

While some countries like the USA have had a slow uptake of prepaid SIM cards, they are the norm in most parts of the world. I prefer to use a prepaid SIM card wherever I am. Here are the reasons why:

- Since I am not locked into a postpaid contract, I can change the provider anytime without any penalties.

- When I am ready to leave the country, I simply use up my prepaid amount, remove my SIM card, and plug in the new country's prepaid SIM card.

- No more nasty surprise phone bills with extra zeros at the end of the month.

- I can pass on my prepaid SIM card to someone else when I leave instead of throwing it out, or I can keep it safe if I plan to return.

Messaging Apps

Messaging apps like **WhatsApp** and **Signal** have become staples for communication and have replaced traditional calling and texting. You can even make real-time voice calls, leave voice messages, and do video calling with others who are on the same messaging app.

Social Media

Sending a good old-fashioned email to share your travel stories with someone is always an option but writing emails is considered of the dinosaur age in the presence of social media giants like **Facebook, Twitter,** and **Instagram**. These have increasingly become the tools of choice for keeping social connections alive with people around the world. **SmugMug** and **Flickr** have long been an accepted platform to share your travel narrative through photos.

Internet Calling

Skype

Skype, one of the first internet calling services, is still around. You can send messages, make voice calls, and video conferences with other Skype users for free—similar to messaging apps. The advantage Skype has over messaging apps is that you can also call a landline or a mobile number even if the person you need to reach is *not* a Skype user. You can call toll-free numbers using Skype from overseas, which you cannot do with messaging apps.

Here is an example to illustrate the point. I have a US Skype account. When I want to reach someone in the USA who is not a Skype user, I dial their number as if from a phone, and the call is free. When I call someone outside the USA (e.g., Germany) who is not a Skype user, I pay a very reasonable international calling charge. When I want to call, let's say my bank's customer support. I can use Skype to call their toll-free number, which I cannot with messaging apps.

Skype/Google number

If you work remotely or have a business in your home country, you will need to maintain a home country number. You can port your existing home country number to Skype/Google and avoid having to give a new number to all your contacts. This way you can use your home phone with a local SIM card since your home country number is now on Skype or Google.

Your boss in the USA will be able to reach you on the same US number while you are on the beach in Australia.

Video Conferencing

A picture is worth a thousand words, but videos convey even more.

There is nothing like being able to see your friends and family while chatting with them! Seeing body language and facial expressions adds a whole new depth and understanding to conversations. **Zoom, Jitsi,** and **Brave Together** provide reliable video conferencing services for a group call. **Google Hangouts** and **FaceTime** (for Apple users) are equally popular.

I prefer Jitsi and Brave Together because they are more secure and private. Plus, they are free to use for unlimited time. Moreover, Jitsi allows free video calling for unlimited participants, unlike Zoom.

My Magic Formula

The world of technology is vast and ever-changing. It is so easy to get confused, overwhelmed, and muddled with so many apps and services out there. Just when you think you have figured out your own magic formula, a better service or app will appear. I am not a big fan of using many digital tools and really, there is *no* need. In fact, it is contrary to the ethos of slow travel. Select a few that you like and stick to them.

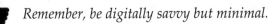 *Remember, be digitally savvy but minimal.*

Here is my small and minimal playlist of apps and tools I use to stay connected while on the road. It has not changed much in the last five years.

Smartphone	Unlocked iPhone bought from the US Apple refurbished store.
Cellular provider	Prepaid plan with T-Mobile when in the USA. Local prepaid SIM card with my iPhone when outside the USA.
Messaging app	Signal: Preferred for personal conversations. WhatsApp: For communication on the road with local vendors, service providers, and with people who don't use Signal. I keep my USA number attached to Signal and WhatsApp even when using the local SIM card in the foreign country. It still works seamlessly and I don't need to give a new number for Signal/ Whatsapp to all my contacts.
Internet calling	Skype to call toll-free numbers, landlines, and mobile phones in the USA and internationally when the person I want to reach is not on Signal or WhatsApp and can be reached only via a landline or mobile number.
Video conferencing	Jitsi (when I am hosting a meeting)
Social media	Facebook, Instagram

The Conscious Slow Traveler

#1 Strike a balance

Yes, it is a marvelous feeling to be able to stay connected with friends and family from any corner of the world. Technology has made it astoundingly easy to send a barrage of photos and live updates instantaneously and anytime. I have often thought of social media platforms as another form of reality TV shows where someone posts an update every half-hour to an hour. At the risk of sounding like a killjoy, I suggest striking a balance between staying connected with your old and familiar world and connecting with the new and unfamiliar world you are now in.

If you divert your time and energy on updating your friends and family with every move you make, you will never be able to sink in and soak up all that is alive around you in your vicinity, waiting to be unearthed. I will also ask you to interrogate—what are you running away from that makes you want to be on social media platforms so often while on the slow road?

Instead, plan focused and intentional times to chat with your family and friends around the world where you are not distracted and can give full attention to the conversation. Treat your slow journey as an evolving mystery novel and post updates weekly, for instance, where each post carries an element of discovery, reflection, and wonder. Give yourself the time and space to breathe in the vibes of the new place you are in and balance it with your need to stay connected with your friends and family.

Chapter 23

Life Is a Trip

*A journey is a person in itself. No two are alike. And all plans,
safeguards, policies, and coercion are fruitless. We find after years
of struggle that we do not take a trip;
a trip takes us.*

John Steinbeck

W e form a relationship with every place we live in, and it
creates a relationship with us. This relationship is rich,
diverse, and dynamic. It changes with time. We wouldn't bare
ourselves to a stranger, would we? It takes time to move from
the surface layer of "Hey, how are you?" to revealing our more
vulnerable self. If a journey itself is a person, then just like a new
person we meet, the place also reveals itself slowly and over time.

It watches us while we explore it. It gauges if we are worthy of
seeing more than what online searches and guidebooks show us.
We have to prove that we will embrace it in all its glory— the
good, the bad, and the ugly. We have to show our commitment to
the land and its people by living there, engaging with them, and
waiting patiently. A trusting relationship begins to develop. Only
then will the place inch further and disclose dimensions that are
unavailable to a holidaymaker.

As human beings, our natural tendency is to revere beauty, like
stunning architecture, fabulous food, good-hearted and friendly
people, and amazing nature. We shun what is uncomfortable or
what we don't want to deal with. But the inconvenient truth is
that each land and its people have a shadow side carved into their
souls due to religious, cultural, and historical reasons or due to
the modern state of affairs. This darker side permeates everyday

life affecting real people. When we come face-to-face with it, it leaves us with unanswerable questions and enigmas.

Why? How could this be?

I don't understand.

At the heart of it all comes a realization that the feelings of loss, grief, anger, resentment, anxiety, panic, regardless of the reason, place, people, culture, beliefs, are universal.

 The tears that we all shed are made of the same stuff.

We find empathy and a real connection. We meet the commonality of our lives through one another and borders dissolve. With these threads of different colored emotions, existence has woven us together into one giant, intricate tapestry. The culture, its beliefs, and its history, through its people, lend tones and cast hues creating vivid bursts of light and shadows of depths in this continually evolving magnum opus.

It is only when we touch the raw, beating heart of that land and its people and recognize it as our own that the initial euphoria of young love (*I could live here!*) transforms into the profundity of real love (*I don't want to leave*). It will beat in your heart long after you are gone, leaving an imprint that will change and enrich your inner landscape forever.

Know that no two will ever be alike. Just like people, each will bring the gift of lessons that we need to learn. While we busy ourselves with sightseeing, socializing, organizing the logistics, going from one destination to another, debating over matters of importance, going to social events, another journey is quietly unfolding behind the scenes — an inward one. This inward journey is the one that creates a tidal shift in our very ideas of living that go deep within us and become a permanent aspect of our life.

 That is what slow travel does. Are you ready?

* * *

If the little girl in pigtails sitting on the verandah railing under the jasmine vine chatting with the moon could peek into her future, she would see herself far away from home in Puerto Escondido, Mexico, typing a full stop right about now. =)

Mind Map Your Way to Slow Travel

Now that you have finished reading the book, it's time to act. When planning, a visual picture is so much better than a dull laundry list. Instead of writing a list of things you need to research, think about and take care of or whizzing them around in your head, I suggest that you draw out a mind map to help you get going.

It's straightforward. All you need are three things:

#1 A large enough piece of paper

#2 A pencil/pen

#3 This book and your thoughts

Then simply begin to draw and jot everything you need to take care of using this book as your guide. If you are technologically oriented, you can use a free tool called MindMeister instead of a paper and pen.

That's it!

Here is a sample mind map I created for my slow traveling in Mexico. You will notice that not everything from this book is on the mind map. That is because some factors were not applicable. Others did not require any research and planning. For instance, there are no vaccination requirements for Mexico. Since I am already fluent in conversational Spanish, I didn't need to think about the local lingo. Create a mind map that is specific to your situation.

In the next section, you will find a Comprehensive Trip Planning Checklist to help you keep track of your travel planning progress.

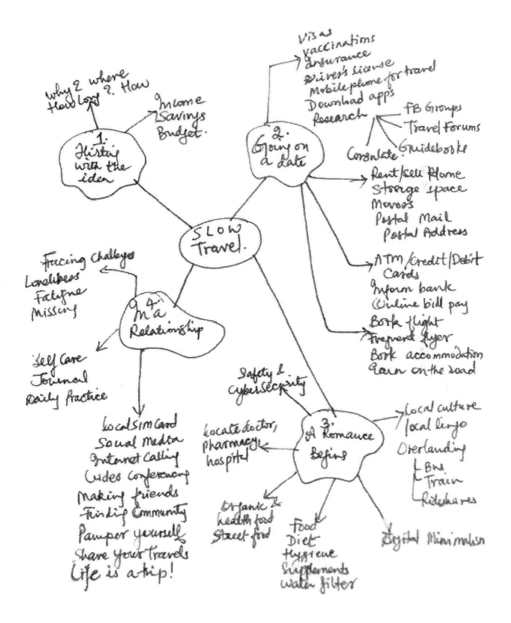

A COMPREHENSIVE TRIP PLANNING CHECKLIST

Items	Yes/No/Not Applicable	Items	Yes/No/Not Applicable
Money Matters Checklist		**Unplugging Life at Home Checklist**	
Budget figured out		Home rented/sold	
Online banking set up		Storage space finalized	
Online bill payments set up		Handling of postal mail sorted out	
New cards researched and applied to		Pet arrangements made	
Bank(s) notified of travel		Neighbors notified	
Fraud alerts investigated with banks		Family notified	
Expiring cards are taken care of		Friends notified	
ATM card withdrawal limits verified		Passport details and a copy left in safe hands	
PIN for all cards set to 4 digits		Copies of important documents made (passport/ driver's license, cards, etc.)	
Do all cards have EMV chips? (preferred)		Movers hired	

Travel Checklist		ID card(s) made	
Passport is valid		Change of address given	
Visa requirements/ application(s) sorted out		**Health Checklist**	
Flight(s) booked		Travel health insur- ance organized	
Train(s) booked		Necessary health checkups are done	
Bus(es) booked		Prescription medica- tions ordered	
Free baggage allowance noted		Supplements/ vitamins/pro-biotics ordered	
Airport transfers organized		Copies of necessary prescriptions made	
Rental car booked		Vaccine require- ments fulfilled	
Other types of transportation organized		Got the vaccination card	
Driver's license is in order		**Digital Checklist**	
International driver's license organized		Laptop/phone/ tablet/iPad make, model, version/serial number noted	
Phone Checklist		Apps downloaded	
Phone unlocked		✿ **Forget-me-not**	
Current phone plan terminated or reorganized			
Important phone numbers saved in phone			

A COMPREHENSIVE PACKING CHECKLIST

Checked-in Luggage

Clothing & Accessories	Yes/No/Not Applicable	Qty	Clothing & Accessories	Yes/No/Not Applicable	Qty
Underwear			Swimwear/Cover-ups		
Socks/Stockings			Coat/Jacket		
Leggings			Rainwear		
Undershirts/Bra			Hats		
Sleepwear			Blouses		
T-shirts			Binoculars		
Dress shirts			Pants		
Casual shirts			Daypack		
Jeans			Small day bag		
Shorts			Gloves		
Dresses			Scarves		
Skirts			Umbrella		
Sweaters/Sweatshirts			Laundry kit (soap, stain remover, etc.)		
Fleece			Walking shoes		
Formal wear			Sandals/flip flops		
Mesh bag			Dress shoes		
Leisure shoes			Belts		

			Ties		
Hiking/athletic shoes			Ties		
Jewelry			Reusable cup		
Purse			Quick-dry towels		
Collapsible totes/bags			Flashlight/ Headlamp		
Sunglasses			Earplugs		
Small lock			Glasses		
Toiletries & Cosmetics			**Toiletries & Cosmetics**		
Makeup remover			Insect/Mosquito repellent		
Feminine hygiene products			Shampoo/ Conditioner		
Birth control			Shaving supplies		
Nail file/ Clippers			Makeup		
Tweezers			Thermos		
Body soap			Moisturizer		
Facial cleaner			Lip balm		
Face lotion/ Gel Cream/ etc.			Toothpaste		
Deodorant			Toothbrush		
Sewing kit			Dental floss		
Hairbrush/ Comb			Contact lenses & solution		
Sunscreen			Toilet paper		
Hand sanitizer					

Health			Health		
Prescription medications			Copy of doctor's prescription(s)		
Important doctors' numbers			Vitamins/Sup-plements/ Probiotics		
Pain relievers			Bandages		
First aid kit			First aid ointment		
Electronics			**Electronics**		
Memory cards			Cables (USB, FireWire, etc.)		
Chargers & batteries			Power adap-tors		
			External hard drive		
Bank & Finance			**Bank & Finance**		
Credit/Debit/ ATM cards			Copies of passport/ cards/driver's license/etc.		
Traveler's checks			Money bag/ belt		
Emergency contact			ID card for checked baggage		
What Can I NOT Live Without?			❀ **Forget-me-not**		

Carry-on Luggage

Items	Yes/No/Not Applicable	Qty	Items	Yes/No/Not Applicable	Qty
Book(s) to read			Important keys (house/car/ storage space/ etc.)		
Light change of clothes			Passport		
Valuables such as jewelry			Money bag/belt		
Cash in USD/Euro			Visa documen- tation		
Credit/Debit/ ATM cards			Driver's license		
Earplugs, eye mask			International driver's license		
Snacks			Accommodation reservations (paper or electronic form)		
Empty water bottle			Insurance cards (travel/health)		
Small toiletry bag			ID card for car- ry-on luggage		
Socks			Copies of passport/cards/ driver's license/ etc.		
Travel blanket			In-flight/journey medications		
Travel pillow			Valuables (jewelry, cash)		
Contact lenses & solution			Copy of doctor's prescription(s)		

Trip itinerary (paper copy/ electronic form)			Prescription medication for the journey		
Hand sanitizer			Vitamins/Sup- plements for the journey		
Tissues			Important phone numbers		
Lip balm			Sunglasses		
Notepad and pen			Sunscreen		
Glasses			Smartphone/ Mobile phone		
Tablet/iPad			Laptop		
Media player			Camera & accessories		
Money bag/ belt			✖ **Forget- me-not**		

ACKNOWLEDGMENTS

*I*t's the people we meet during our slow travel who leave the most significant imprint on us. By that, I not only mean the people we share many moments and become life-long friends with but also the people who cross our paths for a few brief moments. Such as the woman at the fruit-stand that I frequented in the Sunday markets. Or the crystal shop owner who shared his traditional wisdom on stones and their healing potential. Or my aristocratic landlady who often dropped a bag of fruits or vegetables from her garden at my front door. And so many more. Without any of them, my journey and my stories would not be complete.

I want to express my heartfelt gratitude to all the slow travelers, locals, and expats I have had the pleasure to meet along my travel trails, some of whom turned into enduring friendships spanning time and space. You have met a few of them in this book, some with changed names to respect their privacy—Ilaria, Jane, Paula, Antonio, Mia, Juliano, Merle, Matt, Jurgen, Andre, Marijntje, Chrissy, Jim, Ray, Wilca, Jose, Paul, Scott, Pranoto, and Elise.

Others briefly crossed my path, contributed to my slow travel stories, and continue to remain in my memory. You encountered a few of them in this book, with changed names—Ben, Rosa, Martin, Vidya, Jason, Ella, Michael, Antja, Amit, Alex, Lisa, Josip, Anna, and Raffaele.

A big thank you goes to other slow travelers I have not met in real life but have met in the cyber-space. Their valuable experience, understanding, and inputs rounded up this book—John, Jeff, Glen, Emma, Vineeth, Kriszta, Cassi, Amy, and Tamara.

Thank you for reaffirming my faith in the goodness of our human tribe.

ABOUT THE AUTHOR

*B*havana Gesota is an Indian American former technology professional, a life-long slow traveler, self-taught visual artist, writer, and meditator. She was born in India and spent the first twenty-five years of her life in her hometown in Pune before leaving for the USA for work. Over the next twenty-five years, she has lived in nine countries, worked in seven of them, and traveled to twentytwo more over five continents. In 2016, an unexpected health crisis led her to say goodbye to her global consulting business in the technology sector. Since then, she has become a full-time slow traveler while answering the call for creative self-expression.

What brought her to write this book is her firm conviction that slow travel can be a real eye-opener to our very ideas of living through a deep and rich encounter with an unfamiliar culture.

This book is a sum culmination of her own experiences and is meant to help and inspire you to dive into this world and create your own unforgettable travel stories.

STAY IN TOUCH
WITH THE AUTHOR

Wanderlust is contagious. If you have gotten this far, chances are you have it too.

It is impossible to cover the entire length, breadth, and depth of slow travel in one book. There is no full stop in travel, only a paragraph deleted, or a new one added.

You can stay connected with my future publications (travel and non-travel) or updates/supplements to this book by signing up to my mailing list here:

author.bhavanagesota.com/home

Staying true to my desire to be digitally minimal, I will be prudent and minimal in the number of emails I send.

CAN YOU HELP?

Thank You for Reading The Art of Slow Travel!

I really appreciate all of your feedback, and I love hearing what you have to say. Your input is valuable to make the next version of this book and my future books better.

If you have a moment, please leave an honest review of my book at the store where you bought it.

Thanks so much!

Bhavana Gesota

Made in the USA
Columbia, SC
13 June 2022

61708727R00138